Three hungry baby song thrushes are hand-fed
with worms by their foster-parent, the author

Clifford Christie

And then they fly away

Constable   London

First published in Great Britain 1976
by Constable and Company Limited
10 Orange Street London WC2H 7EG
Copyright © 1976 by Clifford Christie
Reprinted 1977

ISBN 0 09 461110 6

Set in Photon Baskerville
Printed and bound in Great Britain by
REDWOOD BURN LIMITED
Trowbridge & Esher

To Joyce

Contents

Illustrations

Acknowledgements

My grateful thanks for making this book possible go to Joyce, my wife, whose total devotion to the birds, beyond all else, has enabled me to recount the successes. Also to Dr Bruce Campbell O.B.E. for giving me the initial encouragement to write the book and his subsequent help at all stages. I am indebted to Ian Buchanan for the illustrations, and the great fun we had taking the photographs, together with the multitude of friends who gave me advice and practical help over the years; especially Trevor and Margaret Easterbrook who would always offer an 'over-spill' home when all our rooms were full. Much of his cine-film, and the two pictures of Royston, the heron, which appear in the book, have also helped me to remember details which may so easily have been forgotten. Donald Platt took the one photograph to remind us of Fishy, the kingfisher – a memorable bird. My children, Lyn, Mike and Alan have always been ready to undertake the many time-consuming chores from fly-catching for house martins to hunting woodlice for lapwings; and of course, finally, I must pay tribute to the birds, the characters in the book, which have taught me so much patience and tolerance.

Photographs by Ian Buchanan are courtesy of the *Banbury Guardian*.

C.C.

Introduction

The war years, for many people, were hard years; a time when families were parted, food was scarce and working hours were long. At four years of age, the outbreak of war had little meaning for me and although I can clearly remember the mass bombing of Coventry and Birmingham later in this troubled period, I was screened from the harsh realities, living, as I have always done, deep in the south Midland countryside where bombing would have had little impact. To me the war meant new friends; evacuees from the industrial cities, alienated from their families and homes to seek the sanctuary of the rural areas. The country children were suspicious at first, many, I am sure, labouring under a false sense of inferiority, and as a reaction to this we often exploited our superior knowledge of the countryside to gain ascendency, scaring the city children with stories of savage bulls, wild pigs and other ridiculously exaggerated tales. Friendships soon strengthened of course and we each accepted the other, but for me, identification with the countryside, which would have been natural anyway, took on a depth of feeling much more intense because of the unnatural circumstances.

This complete association with my environment has never waned. My early attempts to gain a more tangible involvement led to birds' nesting, and even egg collecting – mainly scaling the tall elms and oaks in which the rooks nested to take whole clutches of eggs, for which one of the local farmers paid us a few coppers. Many of the local children, including myself, kept a few ferrets, and the rabbit warrens were well known by the time I had entered my teens – but these were all activities which gave me little real satisfaction and I soon learned that with less noise and more patience, I could become much more closely involved with the inhabitants of the countryside around my home. I began to enjoy watching the badgers on the woodland fringe about a mile from my house, and on more than one occasion we were joined by the barn owls which nested in a nearby hollow chestnut tree, quartering the adjoining field in search of food. From the tadpoles in the lake to the jackdaw nests in the tall elms, I gradually became acquainted with the flora and fauna of that area near the neighbouring village of Thenford, and the path across the fields from my home soon became known to me in every detail.

I could find pleasure and interest from all aspects of natural history but birds fascinated me more than anything else and therefore it followed that, later in life, when the pressures of school exams and technical training had eased, my free time was devoted increasingly to their study. My home in the village of Middleton Cheney, on the Northamptonshire/Oxfordshire border, is situated only three miles from the market town of Banbury, and there I was fortunate to find a very active Ornithological Society. My interest was fostered in an atmosphere of friendship and mutual involvement which formed another significant factor in maintaining, and even strengthening, my early association with the countryside.

Childhood memories are often distorted; prejudiced by the clear recollection of the more enjoyable moments in life whilst the more distasteful features which invade our lives are subconsciously subdued. Summers were always warm and pleasant, autumns mellowed gently into winter and before the full enjoyment of the sunlit snow had been savoured we were back into spring again. Unfortunately the seasons are not so anymore, but life must become a reality at some point and at least I have the privilege of living in the same countryside which provided my playground as a child.

The specific study of birds gave me the opportunity – the excuse even – to retain, with certain modifications, the way of life which had given me so much pleasure in the past. In the village I was regarded as something of a mild oddity – birdwatching being a widely accepted fashion only very recently, but when eventually I married and settled in my present home, I think it was generally regarded that my wife would contribute sufficient sanity to the household to 'save' me. In the event the reverse was true, and over the years our mutual love of birds, and association with them, at least in the eyes of the villagers around us, has led us both into a way of life which can only be regarded as amusingly eccentric. Rather ironically, our lives have been shaped to a great extent, not by any planned preoccupation with birds, although they would always have played their part, but by the actions of the local people who had always looked upon my activities with suspicion.

It is inevitable that on occasions one will find a sick or injured bird – a road casualty, one mauled by a cat, a starving orphan or whatever – and the problem which then has to be faced is what to do about it. Many argue, and I respect the argument, that nothing should be done and that Nature should take her course. For my part I can kill a badly injured bird without compunction because I hate cruelty, but for the people who lived near me there was an easy answer – take it to that 'bird-man' who would know what to do. How wrong some people can be! My love for birds was such that I could not evade the issue, nor even wish to, and my total incompetence did not seem sufficient excuse for not accepting the responsibility which was thrust upon us. We were fortunate, and only over the years have we realized to what extent, in finding a Veterinary Surgeon who was interested in working with birds – the first basic requirement – and I can add to that one other fundamental essential, a wife whose patience and tolerance I have yet to see equalled. This, then, was the basis of our introduction to the many birds which have spent a few hours, days, weeks, or even months with us; temporary phases in their lives which we have endeavoured to make as acceptable as possible. We have tried, and invariably failed, to remain objective in our approach, but I am not ashamed to admit the sheer misery of watching one of 'our' birds die, or the thrill experienced as we watch regained health translated into free flight back to the wild.

1

Reflections on the early days

Our neighbours' cat had been a constant enemy, his attitude to birds and my own being poles apart, when one of our first visitors arrived on the scene. A brood of magpies had fledged nearby, leaving one very small member of the family behind in the nest to perish. The overworked parents just had not the time to cope with such an inferior little fellow when the family dispersed and in this case I took it upon myself to lend a helping hand. With warmth and the security of a cardboard box lined with an old woollen jumper he soon settled down and took titbits of raw minced beef as readily as he would have done from his true parents. Despite his initial weakness he quickly gained strength and confidence and demanded more freedom. His pathetic little wings and ridiculously long legs gave him a most comical appearance but he tirelessly followed Joyce, my wife, as she went about the house and maintained a constant appeal for food. His great delight was to explore the garden and he would wait expectantly, head on one side, ready to pounce on the woodlice under the stones which she used to turn over for him. He grew remarkably quickly and within a fortnight he was testing his wings with real purpose. This made life difficult because he had become so trusting that we feared he would venture out by himself and fall victim to the cat.

He had taken to perching on my shoulder at meal-times, fearing that he might not be present to receive the scraps left on my plate at the end, and when in the garden he would rush back and scramble up to his favourite perch whenever he thought danger threatened. In this way, until he had reached the full flying stage, he managed to survive. This was despite one fairly close shave with his arch-enemy next door. He had been out of the nest for about a month and enjoyed viewing the local scene from the top of a large apple tree: we had therefore relaxed our close vigil on him, confident that he could cope with any situation which might arise. My wife saw him pecking up titbits from underneath the bird-table in the garden when the cat suddenly came into view moving stealthily towards the magpie. She called me and we were both horrified at first but soon realized that before the cat could close the distance to pounce, the bird had moved further away; I am quite sure he was consciously frustrating the cat. After ten minutes or so of cat and mouse (or rather magpie) the cat rushed in desperation, only to watch the magpie lift easily up on to the bird-table top and 'chack' mockingly before flying into the apple tree.

The event was over and almost forgotten by me when, about three weeks later, on an extremely hot afternoon, I was weeding in the garden and saw the magpie drop silently from the tree on to the lawn about ten feet from the neighbours' cat which was sound asleep in the sun. He pranced sideways in a crablike manner towards the cat, standing occasionally to satisfy himself that the cat was still asleep, and when he was actually standing right alongside his old enemy he very carefully gathered a beakful of fur at the tip of the cat's tail and in one swift movement tore the whole lot out. The subsequent sequence of events was too quick to watch, for the cat rose vertically about two feet and all four feet were working overtime before he landed, causing small divots to be lifted from the lawn on contact. By now the magpie was in the apple tree with satisfaction written all over his face and the cat nowhere to be seen.

I am constantly told that birds live in the present, with little thought for the future or memory of the past, but they have to learn many things to survive and given the easy life of partial domestication they have time to employ their powers on less necessary things. The magpie had obviously devoted quite some time to planning revenge on his only immediate enemy. He realized too that hanging around home gave him much more time for pleasure, and although he enjoyed short sallies into the surrounding fields he was never far away at meal-times and preferred to spend the evenings indoors, returning to his tree at dusk.

At about this time a new police constable moved into the village and lodged nearby with my mother whilst the police house was being altered. He was very young, had trained as a cadet in London and was very apprehensive of rural life. His mind was barely put at ease when, on his first visit to my house, he had to share a settee with a magpie but he accepted the situation with resignation and called in the next day in police uniform. He placed his helmet on the table and no one felt at all concerned when the magpie flew over to inspect the shiny metal piece on top; but I think if he could have brought a specific charge against us he would have when, on leaving, he noticed a large white streak right down the side of the helmet. Rather embarrassed my wife cleaned it up and, feeling even more convinced that he had accepted the wrong posting, the policeman returned to duty. The event in itself had been sufficient for all concerned, but the magpie was not satisfied. About four hours later, from the apple tree perch, a shiny-helmeted policeman was seen approaching on a bicycle. From the top of the tree the magpie made a bee-line for the helmet and despite all shouts and much arm-waving he had secured his trademark before flying back to the tree. Unlike the episode with the cat this was not, I am sure, a premeditated malicious attack and I hoped he had completely satisfied himself and would pay no further attention. That was soon proved, however, not to be the case, and the language used on that bird by a certain policeman has no part in this book.

Time passed and similar events and embarrassments heaped themselves one on top of another, but in the late spring of the following year a pair of magpies raised young near the garden and after they had fledged 'our' magpie used to pop down to visit them. At first he was not very popular but gradually he spent more time in the company of the dispersing young and less time at home, until by late summer he had almost deserted us. We left to go on a short holiday and on our return we had lost our companion of many months and he never returned even for a brief visit.

I was sorry in many ways when I realized that he had left for good because he had taught me a great deal about bird behaviour, and although he had posed no real problems in raising him I knew much more about the requirements of young birds – I had watched him bath, feed and preen, I had watched him alert and full of the natural mischief of magpies, and had watched him sleeping peacefully on my shoulder. The bright keen eye, the hallmark of a healthy bird, had come to mean something to me and I had the supreme satisfaction of seeing a near-dead youngster return as a full adult to his natural environment. He would undoubtedly be responsible for stealing other birds' young in the wild, and one might argue that I had done the local avian community a disservice, but life is harsh in the wild and I have never taken it upon myself to make judgements of this nature; I am satisfied if I can return an individual to its rightful place in the world.

In retrospect, looking after the magpie and sharing the early part of his life had been like many aspects of my own early life. There had been no problems, no thought in depth about the subject, merely a pleasant phase to be treated lightly. With the arrival of Beauty, the redstart, however, things changed dramatically and suddenly I had all the problems, frustration and responsibility usually associated with adult life.

There are certain birds which country people know fairly well. They see blackbirds hunting worms on the lawn; watch song thrushes breaking snails on their favourite stone; they see swallows hawking flies on the wing; know the basic diet of the birds of prey and the seed-eating finches, but despite their regular occurrence in fair numbers, many birds remain totally unobserved and unknown. Redstarts, I think, fall into this latter category.

It was around tea-time on 21 August, 1965, that one of the

village lads found Beauty beside the road and brought her along to me. I tried to appear confident as I took the pathetic little creature in my hand – her left leg was crushed and the right wing broken, with a good deal of abrasion on the 'shoulder'. I was tempted to put her painlessly to death but her eyes were bright and I sensed that she was prepared to fight if only given the chance. I made her comfortable in an empty cage, which I covered with a cloth and left her to 'settle in' – a very important part of the treatment.

An hour or so later Joyce and I decided to assess the damage and carry out what repairs were possible. Because of the extensive damage I placed a chloroform pad in the cage sufficiently long to induce unconsciousness without death: an extreme measure and one which I knew could prove fatal. But I could not justify further suffering and I was still not sure that humane death was not the correct course of action. The leg was beyond repair and we amputated it with a pair of clean, sterilized scissors. The loss of a leg does not necessarily hinder a bird in the wild, although of course many species would be rendered helpless in this way. We cleaned the dry blood from the injured 'shoulder' and applied a little Germolene to the exposed wounds. Apart from the leg she looked a good deal better for the clean-up. The whole operation only took ten minutes or so and she was replaced in the cage. After an hour we allowed ourselves a peep beneath the covers and were well pleased to find her alive, her eyes still bright; imagine our joy when, at bedtime, she was standing, rather jauntily, on her one leg.

By morning she was eagerly aware of her new environment and, although nervous, did not object too violently when Joyce force-fed her a few small mealworms followed by a drink from an eye-dropper. Significantly she took water greedily for the first couple of days, but, although there was always a fresh supply available, she did not drink subsequently during her many months with us. That day she ate twenty-two mealworms in all – about half the amount consumed when she was feeding herself – and by nightfall some of the initial tension had eased.

In the morning, however, we were concerned to find that her anus was blocked by dry, powdery droppings: a condition often associated with internal injury. The whole area was bathed clean and zinc ointment applied; at the same time we cleaned more dried blood from her wing and treated this with Germolene. After giving her half a dozen mealworms, we placed her back in the cage for a rest. She was completely undaunted by all the fuss and appeared much stronger at lunch-time; so strong in fact that we stood her on the rim of the dish of mealworms. To my delight she quickly began taking them, so that it was no longer necessary to handle her and risk further damage at each feed. When available, we supplemented her diet with moths and caterpillers, which were all dispatched with little ceremony.

After a couple of days her wing was clean, the final touches delicately performed by Beauty herself; but she was holding it low. So, to ease the burden and allow the muscles to strengthen, the five outer primary feathers were clipped. We should have done this earlier and in all subsequent cases of wing injury it has been standard practice.

Exactly a month later the feather stumps were moulted simultaneously and the new growth could be seen – all very encouraging.

By now winter was approaching and it was obvious that Beauty would not be sufficiently fit to embark on the journey south. Our walks in the country took the form of foraging parties, looking under old dead branches and behind decaying bark for woodlice, centipedes, beetles and spiders, all of which she took with relish. Rather like a dog excitedly anticipating his walk at the sight of his lead, she would flirt her tail and flap her wings when we returned with the spoils. She was now strong on the wing, knew her way around all her favourite perching places, and it seemed merely a question of waiting for spring.

She was a charming little creature; undemanding and affectionate towards myself and my wife although always shy with the dog (an equally undemanding border collie) and my small

22

children, who were a little too boisterous for such a demure female. During the greater part of the day she preferred the security of a large cage on the bookshelf but in the early evening, when the children were in bed, she liked to fly on to Joyce's lap for a few hand-fed mealworms, retiring afterwards to sit on a soft toy rabbit. She loved to settle right down into its pink fur but for what reason I never established. The early winter months passed pleasantly and uneventfully until early February when one of her eyes became cloudy and I had to bathe away the sticky substance from the lid each morning with a lukewarm Optrex solution. She began to lose interest in food and after about a fortnight she died quietly in her cage. I went to a great deal of trouble to find out the cause of death but I am convinced, in the absence of any other evidence, that old age took its course. We were terribly upset because we had started looking forward to her eventual release in the spring, but if my convictions were right she must have spent a happy and eventful life and presumably the migratory trip she had missed would have been her last.

2

Perce

We had spent several long winter evenings analysing the events leading up to Beauty's death; trying to be objective, to determine if, by chance, we had through negligence been responsible for her end, but we had not long to brood before Perce came into our lives. Compared with the delicate little redstart, Perce the lapwing was huge indeed. It was a cold evening when he arrived and he looked miserable and hunched up, blinking at the sudden light – totally opposed to the wondering eyes all around him. He had been found, unable to fly, in a farmyard a few miles away and Glyn, a bird-watching friend of mine, had brought him along to me.

One wing hung limply, although I could detect no damage to the bone structure, and therefore, having placed a hot water bottle and a blanket in the bottom of a large cardboard box, I put him inside to rest in warmth and darkness. He settled straight away and was obviously grateful to be out of the freezing wind which whistled around the house. I had not weighed him but he was plump and obviously well-fed and therefore I did not bother to wake him for food before we, ourselves, retired for the night. We spent much of the night discussing our new 'problem'. As always with a new acquisition we knew little of its food requirements and as Eva Engholm says in her excellent book, *Company of Birds*, it is little value to know that they 'destroy more wire worms, tipulid and lepidopterous larvae, than carnivorous insects and worms' – we just had not any tipulid larvae in the fridge, nor were they in season in my garden as far as I knew.

In the morning he was firmly on his feet but greeted me with a cold, icy stare that only Perce was capable of. His breakfast had to be a rather scratch meal – slivers of sheep's heart which was to have been our lunch. Force-feeding him about half a dozen pieces did nothing to warm his feelings towards me. He did not fight or struggle, nor even attempt to peck at me, he merely maintained a completely frigid response.

His wing was still held very low and therefore we decided that, as with Beauty, we could relieve some of the burden by shortening the primary feathers; even so he insisted on flapping, and I felt certain that there could not be complete recovery unless the wing was satisfactorily immobilized. During the day I worked out a method of placing the wing in a 'sling' and I was anxious to see if it would work, and also if it would be accepted. It was made with soft, anodized, aluminium wire, covered where necessary with soft leather, and kept in place by a clip attached through the feathers. To my delight the wing was held rigidly to the side and obviously caused no pain or anxiety. In all the weeks it remained on, Perce paid no attention to it whatever.

Lapwings are birds of open spaces, glorying in their wonderful acrobatic flight – how could I avoid him becoming totally demented by his enforced captivity? 'Occupational therapy', Joyce pronounced. A corner of the living-room was amply covered with newspaper and he was given a large bowl of water and a tin tray containing soil and earthworms. I watched him: he watched me – so much for the psychological approach! We had purposely set out the paraphernalia in the living-room, partly because one has to share the lives of the birds to appreciate their problems fully, and partly because all of the birds we had kept before had positively enjoyed human, or for that matter canine, company, once they had settled in. Was Perce to be the first notable exception? After all he did wear a continual avian scowl. After a while, however, I felt that he was interested in the soil tray and when eventually he plunged his beak in, I was lucky to see the tail end of the worm disappear. He ate about half a dozen in quick succession and I was greatly relieved to think that I would not have to force-feed him any more; and when he then stalked over to his water dish, drank, and then went to sleep on one leg standing in the water my relief was infinite. The water would keep his feet clean, moist, and in generally good order. Despite the mess, things were working out well.

Bitter frost gave way to milder, wet weather, and each evening, armed with a torch and a polythene dish, I ventured out on to the lawn or the village green to pluck up the worms which were lying out on the surface. It did not take long to acquire about sixty, the needs for an average day, and I was soon back to the warmth of the fire. During the day Joyce would capture a few woodlice and centipedes from under the aubrietia which festoons the little rock bank by the shrubbery, and together with a few mealworms, these gave him a break from the monotony of worms, morning, noon and night.

During the day he spent most of his time standing around, and as soon as dusk fell outside he would become interested in his food tray and water dish. I soon had to add a further shallow tray for bathing, an exercise he greatly appreciated. Perce was very particular about his appearance, using his huge eyes, so useful for nocturnal feeding, to inspect his feet as a finale to his meticulous preening. He stalked around in his corner, never looking other than utterly miserable and the only pleasure he seemed to gain was from the look of horror on the dog's face as he shook water over her after his bath.

As I have said before, he ignored the 'sling' on his wing but we felt very uncertain as to how long it should remain in place. The local Veterinary Surgeon could only hazard a guess but suggested that six weeks would give ample time to repair any muscular strain and, as it was causing no anxiety to the bird, it was advised that we leave it alone for the whole period. Having achieved a satisfactory daily routine, Perce was content if not exactly overcome by joy, but the mild spell of weather was short-lived and as the frost hardened the surface of the ground the worms dived for cover. In desperation I was hacking at the frozen ground on my father's allotment when I realized that I was being watched by one of the keen village gardeners. 'Are you trying to dig?' came the sarcastic comment. I winced with embarrassment and struggling for an equally caustic reply I calmly stated, 'I am preparing this patch for carrots.' A good deal of scathing advice came my way during the next few minutes but then a few flakes of snow stung against my face and he left muttering audibly as he made his way home. Months passed and I had completely forgotten the incident when the same man came up to me and both quietly and grudgingly congratulated me on the quality of the carrots on the allotment. Completely by chance my father had used the same patch and, to my amusement, he had grown the best carrots in the village. The story was completed almost a year afterwards, however, when I saw the old gardener furiously digging in a generous layer of snow – presumably on his carrot patch.

When spring finally came, Perce spent a good deal of time in the garden with us, catching woodlice and various insects and 'shuffling' for worms under the rose bush where the teapot was continually emptied to encourage them. I had spent many hours during the winter months watching this peculiar technique which he regularly employed in his worm dish. He would stand on one leg and thrust the other one forward and then, with his whole body vibrating, he would shuffle his feet across the top of the soil, feeling for worms. When he had located one, his beak was thrust in with unerring aim, and quicker than the eye could follow he had swallowed the worm. I often wondered if this peculiar motion actually attracted worms to the surface but there was never time to ask them once they had been located by Perce.

We could not leave him unattended for fear of cats, and he resented a wire enclosure which I made him so that he could safely spend his day on the lawn. He paced the periphery like a caged tiger and therefore we abandoned this after a few days. We were anxiously awaiting the moult which would enable him to fly again, because his wing had responded well to the treatment and appeared as strong as the other. Should we have shortened the primary feathers? A valid question but belatedly asked, because shorten them we had and until they had regrown he was very definitely grounded. He was obviously enjoying life much more though and it seemed that all would soon be well. But for some obscure reason, diet, shock or whatever, he did not moult until a year later, spending the entire period with us. He never openly resented captivity, as he never fully accepted our company. He remained arrogantly aloof throughout and the odd birds which came and went during his long stay with us were all treated in a similar manner.

When finally he did start to moult, we waited with bated breath to see if the stunted wing feathers would be discarded; by early March he was completely reclad and we decided that he should join some other peewits in a meadow near home which has always been a traditional nesting haunt. Quite typical of Perce, when I placed him on the ground beside the little stream he strode a few paces from me, paused to test his new wing and then lifted easily, flying to join the other dozen or so present, soon indistinguishable among the small flock. I fancied that I could pick out one slightly plumper than the rest – surely he must have a little excess weight after twenty-four thousand worms!

We had greatly enjoyed sharing the company of Perce despite his cold response and our lives appeared empty without him. We tried hard to decide why his moult had been so retarded but his life had been so thoroughly unnatural – no tipulid or lepidopterous larvae, no genuine exercise, no company to satisfy his flocking instincts – nor, perhaps equally important, had his day been regulated by the sun. Admittedly he responded at dusk by feeding and exercising but he was often in a well-lit room for several hours after darkness had fallen. So many factors could have influenced his condition as to make firm conclusions impossible – the only moral appeared to be, 'when it's a lapwing, leave the feathers intact'. In retrospect, I think we could have fed him occasional vitamin tablets which might well have helped, but as yet we have not had the opportunity of testing any of our theories regarding long-stay waders. We did have another lapwing almost straight away, as opposite in her response to us as could be conceived. (Perce had been labelled a male although we could easily have been wrong, and so the other one immediately became female.) She was gentle, affectionate, loved being in contact with Joyce, preferably on her lap, and was in every way adorable. She had flown into something because when she arrived she was concussed and the bottom mandible of her beak was broken, right at the base. Had it been the upper, fixed mandible, we could have successfully clipped it during the period necessary for it to mend but despite all efforts neither we, nor anyone else, could suggest any satisfactory method of effecting a repair. She was naturally unable to feed herself and after three or four days she was quietly put to sleep. We felt absolutely heartbroken and completely incompetent, but we could not allow unnecessary suffering and fortunately the painful end, so often the fate of humans, can be avoided with birds.

The experience with the lapwings had highlighted one fact: birds of the same species can be as different, one from the other, as human beings, and this has been borne out on many occasions since. No rigid rules can be laid down about the care of birds because their individual requirements are so different: one can merely observe, interpret (a bold statement) and respond to the varying demands. They will always give clues as to their state of health and mind if only one is able to draw the right conclusions. To understand a bird is to experience soft feathers against your neck as it settles to sleep (sleep on your shoulder through choice); to watch its excitement mount whilst its meal is being prepared; to have it preen your hair in obvious expression of what we call love; to appreciate a bright healthy eye and so many intangibles, only experienced by those that have truly loved birds and realized that, although they are often motivated by necessity, their behaviour is also complicated and difficult to interpret, but nevertheless, they have more to tell us than is usually accepted.

3

Fred the extrovert and poor Charlie

I spent three and a half years in the prototype division of an aluminium processing company and Fred was born high in the roof of the extrusion plant within the factory. Quite what happened I do not know, but at about three days old he abandoned the nest and fell with an audible thud on the factory floor near one of the presses. An extrusion plant is an inhospitable place for a human being but for a tiny starling it is no place at all. One of the factory hands brought him to the prototype shop, 'where that peculiar bird-man worked', and I popped him into a little box, amply padded with mutton-cloth. He was almost bald with two comical tufts behind the eyes, long gangling legs and protruding belly. I could not see how he could possibly have survived the thirty-foot drop to the factory floor and, worse still, I could see no way such a helpless creature could ever reach maturity.

It was late in the afternoon when he was brought to me and therefore within the hour I was able to recount the tale to Joyce and ask for suggestions. There was little need to ask, for no sooner had the box been placed on the table than Fred's head, beak agape, came over the top and the noise which ensued left little doubt as to his requirements. Again the question, what does one feed a three-day-old starling on? On the bird-table the adults will eat fat, nuts, bread, cheese, bacon, dough, cake, wild·bird seed – in fact, almost anything, but would this hold good for Fred? We had, in the past, successfully raised a fledgling blackbird by feeding him chopped worms, a mixture of crushed sultanas and cheese together with wholemeal bread moistened with milk, and after a brief discussion we decided that

'Blackie's' diet, with a little boiled egg added, would suffice, at least for a while. A little moistened bread was the most easily prepared and soon Fred was 'purring' happily in the bottom of the box, having taken two or three pieces about the size of a pea. This gave us an opportunity to get ourselves better organized. Two cardboard boxes, about a foot cubed, were made ready – each with its own hot water bottle and old woollen jumper. In this way, one bottle could be refilled and the jumper washed and dried whilst the other box was in use, and then a simple transfer of Fred from one to the other ensured that he was always warm and clean. He appreciated the warm woollen jumper but after a short cat-nap he was again wobbling on tip-toes with mouth open wide demanding further attention. It was soon crystal clear that this little fellow had few of the qualities displayed by either lapwing. He was neither demure nor stand-offish – just totally and unashamedly demanding. Like a jack-in-the-box triggered to fire automatically every ten minutes, Fred came over the top of the box. Worms, cheese, bread, small mealworms, tiny pieces of meat fat, a mixture of pulped apple and bread; Fred did not mind as long as it was food and was ad-ministered whenever requested. It must be said that apple and cheese were not given too freely because we did not consider this wise, but Fred's 'taste buds' were not at all sensitive and he gave no indication as to his preferred food. Every bird we have kept, with this very notable exception, has at some stage been choosy about its diet – not so Fred. He only ate small quantities at a time, disappearing into the bowels of the box as quickly as he appeared, but at least our initial problem – how to feed a very young starling – had been solved.

As bed-time approached we wondered what we could do to dissuade him from bobbing up every ten minutes or so like a cork, but when we turned the lights out and placed him on a fresh hot water bottle he settled like a charm. Naturally the bottle cannot be too hot (about the blood-heat of birds, around 107 to 110 degrees Farenheit, is ideal) and it follows that it must not be too cool. This usually entails refilling every two hours

Clifford Christie opens the lapwing's beak
while his wife Joyce inserts slivers of meat

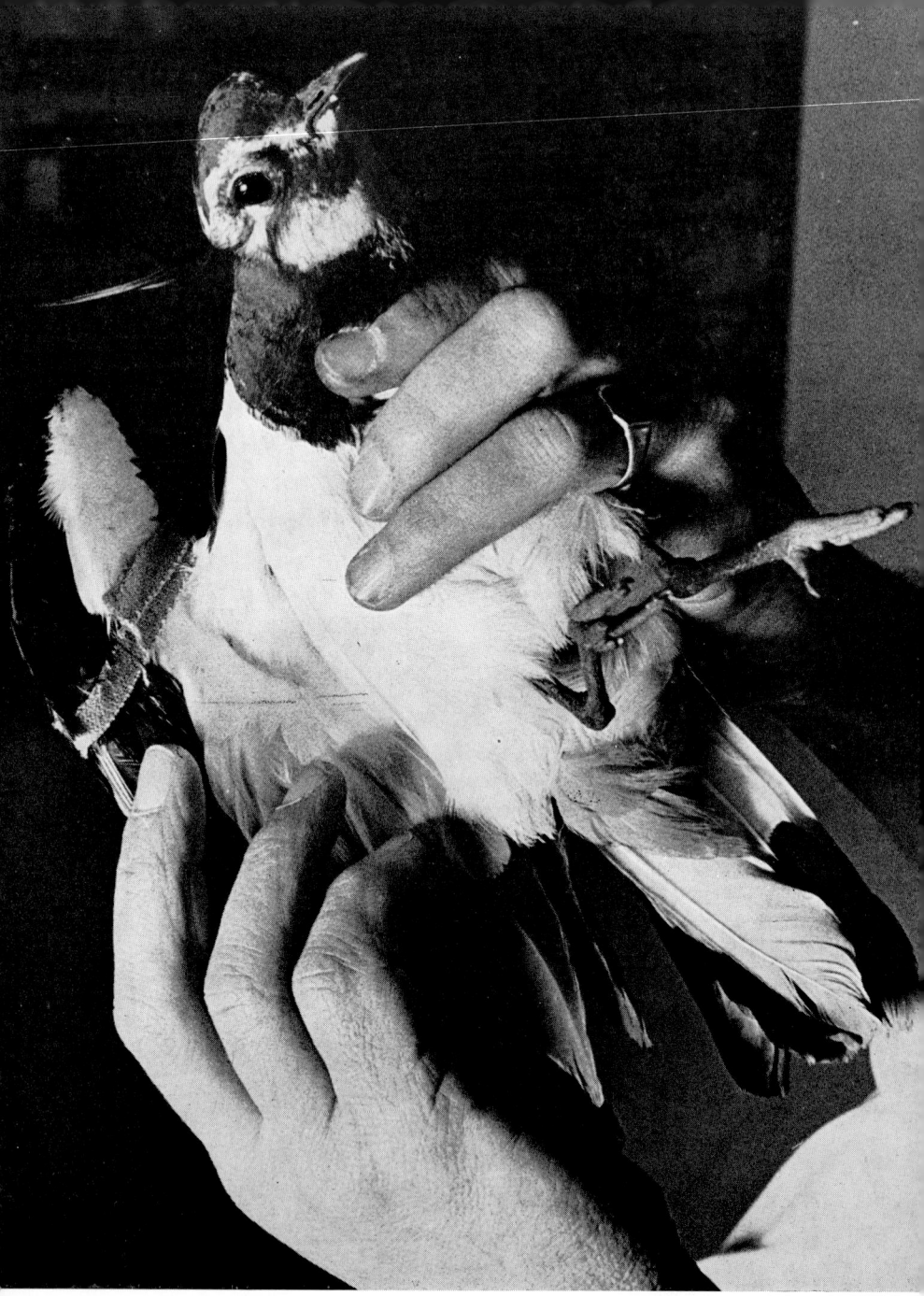

A home-made sling holds Perce's injured
wing in place while the muscles heal

which is no problem during the day but becomes something of a chore during the night, especially with Fred, as he thought day-light had arrived and began his jack-in-the-box act at two o'clock in the morning. The true light of day dawned far too early for me, but for Fred it was the cue to start another burst of joyous activity. I say joyous because he gave the impression that his world was one long round of pleasure. Mischief shone in his eyes and the ridiculous little hairy tufts displayed qualities of the devil himself. It was the hairy tufts which gave Fred his name, after an equally charming and jovial man who lived quite close to us. Fred, the *Homo sapiens*, was completely bald but for a couple of grey tufts just aft of his ears, and his happy twinkling eyes and ready smile bore striking resemblance to Fred the bird – or so we thought.

Fred danced on his hot water bottle like a trampoline expert as I prepared his breakfast and then, having satisfied himself with a few pieces of moist bread, settled down whilst I prepared mine. The toast was barely half done before he was calling for more, and was burned black before he would settle again. This was to typify the first week or so with Fred as a guest. Life quickly began to revolve around this demanding, lovable, little creature. Joyce would hold him in her cupped hands, close to her face and threaten him with violence if he did not behave better and would then immediately gesture a kiss – the type of contradiction quite common in this sort of relationship.

He grew very quickly, having constant attention showered upon him by every member of the family, and after ten days he flatly refused to stay in his box. He wanted mobility and con-stant company and therefore, rightly or wrongly, he could usually be found with either my wife or one of the children, being carried around the garden. He loved to explore under the. shrubs for insects and would scamper around in a frenzy after woodlice if someone lifted a tuft of aubrietia or turned over a promising flat stone. When all else failed, he would wait for the dog to lie down and then scamper up on to her back, impatiently waiting for a ride. She bore this with no ill-will although, given a choice, I think she would have preferred less attention because Fred, inquisitive as ever, would search her hair for insects, probing with his beak, much to Judy's annoyance. Starlings have a habit of probing grass in this manner; the beak is thrust into the grass and then opened, thus exposing any insects hidden beneath, and their eyes are set so that nothing escapes their searching attention.

He loved contact with people and even when he could fly short distances he preferred perching on someone's shoulder, and in this manner he often accompanied us on walks with the dog. Like the magpie, he joined us at the meal-table and it was during one such gathering that Charlie's illusions were first shattered. Fred was just about fully on the wing when Charlie, a half-fledged sparrow, arrived. Any young bird needs a lot of attention as we had just found out, and the newcomer proved no exception. He was prepared to feed himself though and tiny grains of moist brown bread satisfied most of his needs. After a couple of days his droppings became very dry and we knew that this condition must not be allowed to continue and in the absence of any better advice, we gave him a spot of Milk of Magnesia from an eye-dropper. This worked like a charm and we found that we could regulate the consistency of his droppings very easily with no ill effect to him whatever. During the meal-time in question, Fred was ensconced on his favourite perch, my shoulder, and Charlie was in a small cardboard box on the table. Charlie set up a persistent 'I want food' cheep and looked balefully at me, watching every mouthful of food that passed my lips, until, feeling guilty at my greed, I took him out and sat him on my arm whilst reaching for his food tray. He obviously did not grasp the situation for he hopped up my arm, looked at Fred, and uttered a very demanding cheep. Fred's response was instantaneous – he gave him a sharp peck on the head, grasped his leg firmly in his beak and quite ruthlessly tossed the bewildered little thing right over his shoulder. It had all happened before I had chance to intervene, but the effect on Charlie regarding his future relationship with starlings was permanent.

To ensure his safety, Charlie was installed in a spacious cage in the living-room, coming out for exercise only when Fred was otherwise occupied in the garden. Sometimes we would reverse the situation and have Fred indoors and Charlie out, but if all was quiet in the garden and any starlings ventured onto the bird-table, Charlie would scurry for the security of his cage which always accompanied him for this reason. This meant that we had a double problem: a starling that refused to leave us despite the fact that he could find his own food and fly as well as any other bird, and a neurotic sparrow with a 'thing' about starlings. The unusual combination of circumstances presented a most difficult situation and therefore we decided that Fred and Charlie must somehow become friends. They both loved to be hand-fed whilst sitting on Joyce's lap and Fred was not averse to feeding on mine. Each evening, therefore, I fed the starling and Joyce fed the sparrow and by manoeuvring the chairs, and finally sitting together on the settee, we managed to get them feeding amicably together in close proximity. The climax came after about a fortnight when Joyce finally managed to feed them, one on each leg. They did not become close friends and live happily ever after in story-book fashion, but to a great extent Charlie conquered his neurosis and Fred became sufficiently tolerant to control his temper.

I could understand Charlie's distrust for Fred, and to an extent, Fred's resentment of Charlie but it was about this time that we realized that all birds tried to shun the company of my mother. She lived close to our house and was a constant visitor, and when 'our' birds flew or ran to their box or the remotest corner of the room as she entered, we always assumed that they distrusted the intrusion of a comparative stranger. My mother loved birds and always felt hurt at their response but, being a kind, sensitive person, she never forced her attention on them. Fred was usually an exception to any previous rule, and loved the company of all and sundry who cared to breeze in – unless it happened to be my mother. He would then dive for cover in any suitable dark corner and nothing would induce him out. This behaviour among birds remained constant right up to my mother's death and no one has been able to offer any reasonable explanation, although several people have witnessed the strange phenomenon.

The very close association, essential when birds are young and entirely dependent upon their foster parents, naturally relaxes as they mature. It is the process of evolving their independence which is often very difficult. In the case of Fred, the transition period between dependence and independence was a very long one: the same had held true for the magpie earlier on. There are many risks involved, if birds become too trusting, when exposed to the many hazards experienced in the great outside world and in all subsequent cases we have gone to great lengths to develop their more natural instincts as part of the growing-up process.

Whether or not Fred would have ever deserted us entirely I am not sure, because although he spent many hours out of our company he maintained daily contact and was always present on my shoulder before I entered the house in the evening on return from work. He would come in with me, sit tight whilst I glanced through the newspaper, wait patiently throughout dinner, and then descend my arm to finish off the titbits left on my plate for him. He would then resume his perch and wait for me to finish off my coffee, hoping for the usual stroll round the garden. At this stage, if we took the dog for a walk, he would accompany us for about half a mile but then he would fly back home and we might, or might not, see him again that day.

Holidays were always difficult to arrange because we could never predict the situation much in advance and no one I knew was prepared to take on the responsibility of caring for even the easiest cases. But with Charlie and Fred both capable of fending for themselves, we decided that, if we asked my mother to open the kitchen window each day to let them in if they wished, we could take a few days break by the sea. We naturally wondered what their response would be and deep down we felt many misgivings, but the children had to be considered and with little feeling of real guilt we enjoyed four or five days of complete freedom. On our return our thoughts turned immediately to Fred and Charlie – not a sign; no friendly greeting; not even a fleeting glimpse. Guilt and dismay welled up inside us. It was early evening when we returned and Fred, at least, should have been on hand to see what was being offered at the meal-table or to wait for a turn round the garden. By nightfall we had seen nothing of them and we fell asleep, greatly troubled by our thoughts. In the morning I looked out of the bedroom window and immediately saw Charlie on the bird-table – I called and he looked up, but showed little recognition and carried on pecking at the food. As soon as I was dressed I went out into the garden and held out my hand for Charlie to hop on, but with a scornful look he flew into an elder bush in the adjoining field. Feeling hurt I wandered across the lawn and excitement mounted when I spotted Fred in the apple tree, 'Maggie's' favourite look-out. I was horrified when I received the same response from him, but from that day, although they were often in the garden, I never regained their confidence. I had turned my back on them and I had paid the price. Even Judy, the constant subject of Fred's interest, was never approached again, for in these brief few days they had become totally wild and unresponsive. Perhaps it was the best thing which could have happened, but I have rarely been slapped down so convincingly in my life before or since.

4

Success and failure

The breeding season was in full swing when we returned from the few days' holiday. This is always a dangerous period for the hordes of young, innocent birds making their first acquaintance with the hazards of life beyond the nest, and it usually follows that it is a busy time for my wife and me. Within hours of our return we were confronted with a completely new 'problem' – a fledgling swift.

The two main breeding colonies of swifts in the village are in the old church, about a mile from my home, and under the eaves of a group of pre-war houses which constitute The Avenue, situated mid-way between the church and my house. The tiny heap of sooty feathers in the hands of one of the village lads had come from the church colony, and it must have taken a fearful tumble because its wings were barely half-grown. But for the fact it was so light it must surely have dashed itself to death on the ground below. I took it from the lad willingly and it was not until he had disappeared from sight that I realized the gravity of the situation. 'We've had nothing like this before,' I ventured to my wife. 'What do we do with this one?' The initial action had, by now, become automatic and the little chap was soon settled into a warm box whilst we collected our thoughts. Analysing our knowledge of swifts' requirements was not a long job because the fact that we knew they hunted for food on the wing hardly helped the present situation; that they reputedly sleep on the wing was equally useless knowledge because we knew that in fact they rested on ledges. 'That may be helpful,' we thought. We could not see how it could be, but 'it may be'!

Mealworms are always useful; fully-grown ones for the

larger birds and young tender ones for the smaller birds. Blowfly maggots from the fishing-tackle shop are sometimes invaluable, although they have a nasty habit of hatching out too quickly and, although I have never been successful with it, it is possible to purchase dried insects and proprietary brands of insect food substitutes. The need for food is always pressing with young birds, although swifts have an incredible ability to endure periods without food; but we were anxious to establish whether our new charge was injured or not and test his response to food.

Our first reaction was one of relief for there appeared to be no evidence of injury and therefore we anxiously prepared his first meal. I was to place a small amount of insect substitute from the end of an eye-dropper into the mouth which Joyce was hopefully going to open. With practised fingers, she gently opened the delicate soft bill which revealed an astonishingly large cavity. With slightly less confidence I managed to deposit the food right into the back of his mouth, Joyce released her hold and we waited for him to swallow – he spat it out! He rejected the food so positively that we felt a repeated attempt would only draw the same result. Perhaps it was too cold. Regurgitated food would presumably be at body temperature and in any case, the appearance of the adult at the nest would stimulate food-begging which would make the job easier. Neither my wife nor I resemble a swift in any way whatever and we could think of no way of disguising the eye-dropper which we hoped to use as a food dispenser. Perhaps a few pulped mealworms would simulate the correct diet more closely and bring about a more satisfactory reaction. Perhaps – but they did not! 'We could possibly swat a few house flies,' Joyce added in desperation. This we proved we could do. What we could not do was persuade the bird to eat them. A few drops of water might produce the stimulus necessary to start feeding? He was certainly not averse to water and accepted a few spots willingly but solids continued to go one way – out again, promptly.

During the frustration of trying to feed him, another problem had come to light. With his very short legs it was inevitable that his body would soon become fouled by his droppings – the underside of his tail was already smeared white. It appeared a hopeless situation and we were filled with despair as each effort to get food inside him failed. He was a perfectly healthy bird and we could not allow him to fade away because of incompetence, nor could we replace him in the nest high in the church steeple, because it would be particularly inaccessible.

Looking around the room for inspiration I thought that he might feel at home in the space between the ceiling and the curtain rail if I folded the ruffle of the pelmet strip back to form a soft ledge. There was a gap of some three inches and when I placed him on the ledge he shuffled in and settled comfortably, obviously approving of his new-found home. I had read somewhere that small slivers of liver formed an ideal substitute for an insect diet and so, without hesitation, Joyce set off with renewed hope to the local butcher's shop. Mick is a long-suffering friend and expects to be asked for the weirdest things for our birds, and therefore a couple of ounces of liver was very much in order. I stayed behind to watch the bird but he was too pleased to be 'back home' to do anything but sleep.

When Joyce returned we again pondered how best we could induce liver into a bird which obviously was not going to cooperate. His beak was so soft and pliable that we feared that we might damage it if we tried too many unsuccessful attempts, but on the other hand there was no artificial heating in his new quarters and without food he would soon become cold, weak, and die. About an hour had passed since our last attempt to feed him and we had decided to try again, when he shuffled to the edge of the 'nest', excreted over the side (all very sanitary), and then scrambled down the pelmet using his very powerful claws squeaking frenziedly. 'Food-begging,' I said excitedly and cut a tiny slice of liver about half the size of my thumb nail. He clung to the curtain, squeaking with beak wide open, and when Joyce offered the liver he swallowed it with relish. Three times in quick succession he took similar amounts before he

scrambled back to the nest, settling down and purring contentment. I have rarely felt the degree of relief I experienced then;
we really felt that we had turned the corner.

We sat down to discuss the situation, feeling concern for his
welfare during the night now that the immediate difficulties
had been resolved. It would be impossible to use the hot water
bottle technique and we could think of no better solution than
to work shifts during the night, remaining in darkness in the
hope that he would sleep, but present in case of emergency. Our
discussion was cut short, however, after about half an hour
when he emerged once again, clawed his way down the pelmet
strip, squeaking for food which he accepted as readily as before.
About three tiny pieces of liver was sufficient to send him
scrambling back to the security of the nest, but it was too easy to
be true. We soon found that his calls for food were audible, even
in adjoining rooms, and therefore the close vigil was not absolutely necessary. Nor did the night period present any problems. He slept soundly until first light – and presumably any
self-respecting swift is ready to be fed at five am – and as the
droppings were still firm and chalky white I gave him a few
spots of water. I can only assume that swifts in the wild are
denied the 'tea in bed' routine but he took water greedily and it
appeared to do no harm.

The only major question which was still to be answered
regarded his eventual release. When the young are ready to
leave the nest, they are obviously induced to fly either by starving them out or by some other stimulus, but if he suddenly felt
the need to fly he would be too restricted and would be in
danger of damaging his incredibly long wings. There was no
ready answer to this problem though and therefore it had to be
shelved for as long as possible. Meanwhile Joyce had become
extremely fond of 'Squeak' and as a change of routine she would
have him on her lap for an hour or so in the evenings to sponge
his beak clean and ensure that the blood from the liver was not
fouling the feathers at the side of his face. He appeared to enjoy
this wash and brush-up, and before long he was helping out

with a quick scratch with his claws and began to establish a preening routine, carefully inspecting his wings, tail and feet. At this period of the day we used to sit with the kitchen windows wide open and the electric light on to encourage moths in. It was a barbaric business but Squeak associated his periods on my wife's lap with a juicy moth or two and, as quickly as we could swat them, he could eat them. One evening a particularly large moth ventured in and when I offered it to Squeak I felt rather ridiculous because the moth looked as large as his head. A hungry swift saw this as no problem at all, however, and when he opened his beak it looked as though the lid of a box was opening on its hinges: a second later there was only a bulging crop to prove that he had eaten it. After a meal like this he would sit for a few minutes and then scratch his wings, fluff his feathers and resettle in blatant content.

As the days passed he would spend more and more time stretching and wing-flapping but he was always ready to go back to his nest and only abandoned his ledge to call for food. On the tenth day however, I returned home from work and Joyce said that he would not go back to the nest but clung to the curtain throughout the day. This, then, was the moment of truth. Apart from his extensive white chin and pale breast he was a mature swift and ready for the world outside. There was no point in delay for he would never be in better condition and the sky outside was full of martins, swallows and swifts feeding on the plentiful insects which abounded in the warm afternoon sun. With a great deal of apprehension, always associated with this occasion, Joyce carried him into the garden. He sat on her hand flapping, his claws raising the skin on the back of her hand as he ran up his engines with the brakes on prior to take off. For what appeared an eternity he tested his wings and then quite suddenly he was off – across the field at the bottom of the garden; a steep climb to rise over the big oak tree at the bottom before levelling out to join the other dots in the sky darting after insects. Even with binoculars it was soon impossible to deter-mine which of the screaming throng was ours, but he was on his way and it would have been improper to ask any more than he had given us.

Squeak's short but exciting stay had successfully filled the gap after Fred's decision to leave and we looked forward to a few days respite to catch up on the work in the garden and home. Living on our nerves, as is often the case when taking on the responsibility of caring for sick or injured birds, can prove quite exhausting and therefore a period of relaxation is always welcome. The period was to be short, however, as a few days later, on 17 July, Moses arrived and despite all efforts a major failure was to follow.

Moses was a little moorhen chick; so called because he was found among the bullrushes. When I first set eyes on him I knew a tragic mistake had been made for he was a lively little chap about two days old and although he may well have strayed further from his mother than was good for him, he certainly was not orphaned as the benevolent fisherman who 'rescued him' thought. He came to me through a third person and sadly I did not know the location where he had been found and apparently the fisherman was off on holiday – it was a truly bad start but we had to make every effort to amend the situation.

It was about four-thirty pm and we took him hopefully to a small pond nearby in my father's garden, to see if he would peck food from the surface. I have watched young moorhen chicks for hours on a local lake and although it is difficult to establish what they are pecking at on the water surface, they always appear busily active, and natural feeding is always infinitely preferable to substitute foods. He took to the water, bobbing like a little cork, but soon scrambled on to a water-lily leaf where he stood looking rather pathetic. We launched him again, this time poking at the water with a finger to try to interest him in the aquatic insects which were present in profusion, but he made a bee-line for his water-lily leaf and clambered on, using his little flipper-like wings and tripping over his ridiculously large feet. He stood like a shipwrecked sailor, so we gathered him up and placed him in a small box on a hot water bottle which we liberally covered with soft dusters. My daughter donated a cuddly panda (in theory the right colour) for him to snuggle under and we left him for about half an hour to warm through. As soon as he became restless, a wobbly little head supported by even wobblier legs emerged from beneath the panda, and I tried to feed him a little dried daphnia mixed with water from an eye-dropper. He did take a few spots but the exercise was far from satisfactory and so we decided to try him with a few very small earthworms. I found several tiny worms in the garden, coiled into tight balls in the dry earth and I thought that we had probably hit on the right idea at last. I was even more encouraged when we managed to force-feed him half a dozen. After his feed he was ready for bed and settled contentedly among the warm dusters.

At about eleven pm we repeated the feed, settled him on a fresh hot water bottle and went to bed, setting the alarm for two am when the bottle would need refilling. It had become a standard procedure all too familiar, and yet for some obscure reason the alarm failed to rouse us, and I woke with horror to find that it was already six am. Fearing the worst, I dashed downstairs to find that he had clambered out from beneath the panda and sat cold and weak in the corner of the box. I warmed him in my hands until I could feel his strength returning and then, with the help of Joyce, I gave him three small worms. He appeared none the worse after half an hour on a freshly filled hot water bottle, but I was cursing myself for the blatant negligence during the night. Tiny chicks cannot survive periods of cold and he should not have been exposed to such a risk. I was worried when I left for work but when I returned at lunch-time Joyce said that he had eaten fourteen tiny worms during the course of the morning and had even taken a swim on my father's pool. She had failed to induce him to feed from the surface of the water but he was looking perky and she said that he had excreted whilst swimming on the pond, so it appeared that the worms were being digested and we felt very much more hopeful.

After lunch we took him for another brief swim; convinced that he would have to take to the water if we were going to be successful in raising him. My son, always in attendance if there is a chance to play with water, caught a couple of water-skimmers to feed him. I lifted him out of the water on my hand and placed one of the insects in his beak. He half swallowed it but then immediately regurgitated it, together with a couple of worms he had been fed a few minutes earlier. Thinking that he had probably been overfed, we returned him to his box where he slept for the rest of the afternoon.

His supper consisted of a few spots of 'diluted daphnia' but he appeared warm and active whilst on my lap and returned again to his box willingly. When I was ready for bed (with a stand-by alarm clock to ensure waking for the bottle change) I wrote in my notes, 'Still *very* young and vulnerable and every hour will be critical for the next few days.' These words were painfully true.

I do not wish to bore the reader with unnecessary detail but a straight reading from the 'log' for 19 July – the third day – indicates several points which only become obvious after the event.

05.00 hrs   Changed water bottle and fed him two tiny worms washed down with a couple of spots of dried daphnia in water. Appeared stronger than yesterday morning.

08.15   Two small worms dipped in moist daphnia.

11.00   Fed as 08.15; changed hot water bottle.

14.15   Fed him worms but he rejected them so fed him just daphnia – pecked off the end of an eye-dropper.

16.15   One small worm and daphnia.

19.30   Taken to pool for swim. Took a fly from my finger which I caught on the surface and then three pieces of wet, very fine grass roots and algae which had grown into the water. Each piece was about twice the size of a grain of wheat. Brought him back and he pecked a little daphnia from the eye-dropper. Filled his bottle and put him to bed.

22.30   Offered him some weed which he didn't want. Took a small worm and daphnia from the eye-dropper. Filled his bottle and put him to bed.

I was worried when I looked back over the events of the day because he was obviously not taking sufficient food. Was it because his health was failing or was it because we were offering the wrong types of food? Both Joyce and I thought that it was a combination of the two: the latter, in fact, causing the former. He would peck at daphnia from an eye-dropper and eat small amounts of weed but he would not be induced to take food naturally on the pond.

We decided that he should be fed as often as possible, if necessary working shifts, and that I was to get up at two-thirty am to begin my stint. The idea was to keep him warm in his box in order to utilize his food as efficiently as possible, and to feed him whenever he woke up. We could not think of a better food-source than daphnia and weed, although I am sure that we were obsessed by the early success when we tried this and did not pay sufficient attention to trying other alternatives. After all, the swift had responded remarkably well to liver and had maintained a steady growth rate.

He did not eat very much during the night but this did not worry me as I considered that the rest was as essential as food, and he would not be fed during the hours of darkness in the wild. Shortly after seven am Joyce took over nurse-maid duties and he tried to peck imaginary food from her skirt when she placed him on her lap to give him his breakfast. This greatly encouraged us, although he did not appear too keen when offered weed, but he did peck encouragingly at the daphnia on the eye-dropper. During the day he was fed almost constantly, and in the afternoon Joyce took him over to the pool for his swim. He scorned the safety of the water-lily leaf and pecked among the marsh marigolds growing at the waterside. He took a couple of worms and a few pieces of algae before my wife brought him home for a warm in the box. Both Joyce and Moses were very cheerful when I arrived home after work and we felt much more confident that we had adopted the right tactics. During the day he had taken more food, more exercise and was generally brighter altogether.

How quickly can one forget one's own words of wisdom: 'every hour will be critical for the next few days.' That evening Joyce and I had to leave the house for about three hours to visit a friend. We debated whether to take him with us in his box or to fill his hot water bottle and leave him settled at home. We opted for the latter, feeling sure that no harm would come to him in the circumstances. We drove off cheerfully, discussing the very positive progress made that day and although prepared to admit that we were not over the hill, we had little doubt that we could cope with the situation. I chatted to my friend, Royston, about the problems of feeding Moses because he is a very experienced field ornithologist, hoping that something useful might come out of the conversation, but a moorhen chick at home is so very different from the little black ball with 'frosted' head which bobs alongside mum on the lake, busily choosing food and apparently impervious to the cold, damp surroundings. But things were under control now and the conversation was lighthearted before returning home.

A deep feeling of guilt took hold of me when I peered into his box. He had been fed almost continually during the day with minute portions at a time, and he had obviously hopped out for food shortly after we had left him. He now sat dejectedly in the corner of his box and felt cold to the touch. How many times had I taken him in my cupped hands, offering the warmth of my body to keep his tiny heart beating? More importantly, how many times had the necessity been my fault? Certainly this time, and the realization made me feel sick inside. The warmth soon revived him and he took a small worm, some weed and a little daphnia but the enthusiasm to feed had gone again.

During the night he was restless but he was not interested in

47

food and by four-thirty am his breathing had become irregular. Shortly afterwards, each time he inhaled he made a 'clicking' noise which caused us terrible concern. I held him in my hands and he settled to sleep, and there he remained until morning. We felt desperate, useless, and utterly guilty. We racked our brains to try to find a solution and Joyce suggested trying a little Complan to nourish him. She mixed a little into a thick paste and he pecked some from the eye-dropper. He spent the whole day with Joyce, sleeping on her lap with her hands cupped around him, and took small amounts of Complan regularly. His breathing became less laboured and by lunch-time he was uttering the occasional contented 'cheep' in his sleep; reminiscent of the early days when he first arrived. We were far from happy but he had survived the day and taken some nourishment – the night would be the telling period. I was feeling tired through lack of sleep but I was determined not to let up now and in any case my feeling of guilt was still too strong to allow me to sleep properly.

The final entry on my notes sums up that night better than I could describe long after the event: 'Sat up with him through the night and held him in my cupped hands – his breathing again became laboured. At 03.05 on 22/7 he finally died in my hands, he just stopped breathing.'

I have learned a tremendous amount from the experiences with Moses, I hope sufficient to ensure that the results would never be repeated, but I was too overcome by emotion at the time to analyse the reasons for his death. I merely placed him in his box and went to bed – I did not speak to Joyce, there was no need. Even in the morning we could find no words for conversation, it appeared pointless and futile; a totally indescribable feeling.

Fishy the kingfisher was never really
happy out of his box

The tawny owl, Olly I – a bundle of
grey downy feathers on arrival

5

A jewel from the stream

All birds that we had come across needed water to a lesser or greater degree but, living in a Midland area where agriculture still dominates the scene, it was natural that most of the birds brought to us would be land birds, living and feeding in the fields and small woods surrounding us. For us, none of the storm-tossed coasts and gale victims so intensely described by Dorothy Yglesias in her book *The Cry of a Bird*, in which she wrote about the bird hospital established on the Cornish coast by herself and her sister. In fact we are lucky in that the sheer numbers of victims following disastrous conditions at sea are never encountered by us, and the birds arrive more in a steady trickle than a mass influx.

We have our share of water-birds, however; dabchicks, great crested grebes, moorhens and coots nest on many of the canal reservoirs which feed the Birmingham/Oxford canal which runs north to south about three miles to the west of my home. The route of the canal closely follows the valley of the river Cherwell and where this valley is subject to winter flooding it offers refuge and food for many waterfowl from late November through to March. Sizeable flocks of wigeon and teal seek sanctuary here, and they are joined by mallard, pintail, shoveler, mute, Bewick's and whooper swans in variable numbers. In autumn and spring the passing migrant waders drop in to feed and rest and a few pairs of curlews and redshank remain to breed in the lush meadows.

It is not an area of imposing grandeur; even the streams and river glide quietly through the meadows, the mud-lined banks and silted beds, channelling the water towards the sea

49

in orderly fashion. Not far away, among the Cotswold hills, the music of water can be heard tumbling along shallow, rocky streams and grey wagtails can be seen flitting nimbly from stone to stone but 'my' grey wagtails can only be found near the occasional mill lasher or artificial waterfalls constructed in some of the larger gardens which bear the stamp of Capability Brown.

We have woods, not forests; ponds, not lakes; but it is this tremendously variable mosaic which makes this part of the Midlands such a wonderful place to live. It has dignified charm – primroses and anemones embroider the woodland carpet, violets and celandines adorn the warm hedgerow banks, but nothing dominates. Sadly, of course, the latter statement is only true if we exclude man's activities, but even so a true 'Midlander' is very jealous of the area in which he has been privileged to establish himself.

This is, of course, kingfisher country. On one walk from Kings Sutton along the canal towpath down to North Aston, Joyce and I saw no less than twelve individual birds, skimming the water like jewels in the sun. It was, therefore, almost inevitable that a kingfisher should feature in our list of birds.

The arrival of birds at home is so absolutely unpredictable that one can never really prepare. For one thing, there is usually no time to consider the next arrival because each individual demands so much time and mental attention that absorption in the immediate problem is absolute and hence anything in the future must wait its turn. The lack of preparation has never been more apparent than it was when our kingfisher arrived. It was on 28 June, 1972, and we had arranged to visit some friends in the village for an evening meal – a rare occasion indeed – and after a scratch lunch at midday I was hoping to tidy the garden during the afternoon (another rare occasion), it being a particularly pleasant day. The telephone rang and a schoolteacher from a village some twenty miles away spluttered out her story rather apologetically, of how four small boys from her school had just brought in a near-dead kingfisher which they

had found beside a local stream, unable to fly and fully unconscious. She was dressed ready for a wedding which she was to
attend some fifteen minutes later and there was a considerable
degree of urgency in her voice. After a little deliberation it was
decided that she should place the bird in a small cardboard
box, on an old woollen jumper, where it could rest in darkness
and warmth whilst she dashed off to make her apologies to the
bride and groom. She left with the promise that she would be at
my home with a minimum of delay. This gave me time to make
similar apologies to our friends who had already gone to considerable trouble over the meal preparations, but they were
very understanding and agreed that priority must be given to
our awaited arrival.

The first flurry of activity over, we had to decide on a plan of
action to deal with such an unfamiliar bird. We had watched
them fishing for minnows in the river and the small streams
near home, but how could we possibly set up adequate quarters
at home for such a guest? We had not long to deliberate, however, before a car drew up outside the house and out scrambled
the four boys, each with eager eyes focused on the cardboard
box carefully carried by the school teacher. My first reaction
was of relief that the bird was, in fact, still alive, but when I
peered in and saw him lying helplessly on his side, my heart
sank. He looked so tiny and even his 'sparkle' was gone. The
feathers were dishevelled where the boys had carried him in
hot, sticky hands. His eyes were closed and I could not even
detect the rise and fall of his feathers to establish that he was
breathing.

The school-teacher looked dejected and asked if he was dead.
I picked him up gently and held him in my cupped hands; the
added warmth from my body brought a tiny responsive movement but he was almost gone. I had to tell them that there was
little hope but one of the lads remained confident that we could
breathe life into him and, hoping that some of his confidence
would soon rub off on to me, I watched them depart. We could
offer no immediate help other than constant warmth and rest,

but these being the two great healers, we still had hope. Joyce made him comfortable on her lap and held her hand cupped over his body; there was no responsive movement this time but she could just feel the feeble and irregular movement of his breathing. For two eternally long hours he lay in this position. His breathing at first gained regularity and later, greater depth and at the end of this period he shuffled his feet up under his body and generally arranged himself into a more comfortable position.

It was by now early evening and our experience with Moses had taught us not to relent, even for a moment, in the joint struggle for survival. I got a dish of water and, having dipped my finger in, allowed a spot to trickle into his beak. I could see the little feathers at the base of his chin move in a swallowing action so I repeated this a couple of times. He briefly opened an eye and settled again to sleep. This time was different, however, this was genuine sleep, sought out of tiredness not forced by coma, and we felt considerably relieved. He shuffled into a more comfortable position from time to time and at ten pm, after five hours of warmth and rest, he lifted his head and looked around him with uncertain eyes. I had desperately sought food for him during this period but on a Saturday evening with no shops open, anything resembling fresh fish was completely unobtainable. As a last resort I thawed a frozen fish finger which I had found in the refrigerator and gently placed a small piece, about three quarters of an inch long and of pencil thickness, into his beak. He did not object and tried to swallow but he was too weak even to accomplish that and I had to stroke his chin to help it down. Having swallowed it, he appeared a little perkier and I was grateful that the effort on his part had not proved fatal. A few minutes later I was encouraged to try him with another piece of cod of similar size, and this time he managed to swallow himself. After he had taken a third piece I decided that he should rest again and he was pleased to snuggle back under Joyce's hand. An hour later he shuffled out again and took a similar feed – this time swallowing without effort and throwing back his head to ease the passage of the fish down his throat. It was certainly the first time in his life that he had ever eaten cod, but he appeared to accept it readily and the situation was improving all the time.

Joyce and I were by now both tired and hungry and so Fishy was placed gently into a box using the hot water bottle technique. He settled straight away – he must have suffered a terrible ordeal because he was still completely exhausted. He remained in his box all night, but for the bottle change period, and breakfast-time found him still very weak. He was ready for a drink again, though, and took several spots of water from my finger, followed by three pieces of cod. The easiest way to feed him was to place him in a little 'nest' in Joyce's lap so that he was fully supported and from where he could stretch his neck to swallow; this, apparently, was essential for the operation to be satisfactorily achieved. His day was spent mostly in his box and he came out for five separate feeds, all similar in quantity, for as yet we had no way of judging his requirements and we were hopeful that he would soon be strong enough to give us some indication.

Our main attention now was beginning to focus on methods of feeding and housing him which were more closely akin to those found in the wild. Obviously we had to wean him off cod and on to minnows, but how this was to be achieved I still had little idea. I consulted my friends as to methods of procuring minnows, and one particular friend, Mick, who had spent his childhood near the river, recounted how, as a lad, he had caught ample supplies in a baited jar which he tossed into the river at suitable places. It all sounded too easy. A sweet jar with a hole about an inch diameter pierced in the screw-top, baited with bread paste and secured to the hand with a piece of string, was sufficient, apparently, to catch all the minnows I would require – however many that might be! He even provided me with the jar in which to catch the minnows and that evening my daughter Lynda and I drove off to the nearest brook to stock up.

We gazed into the water as we walked along the bank, looking for our first shoal. 'Perhaps they are hidden in the reeds near the banks,' she said, after we had covered about a mile without catching sight of a single minnow. We placed the jar hopefully in the water and left it whilst we wandered on to see if the minnows were congregating under the road bridge further along – nothing. Near the bridge the bed of the stream is covered by large stones, so we started turning some of these over in search of aquatic life. A few freshwater shrimps skimmed off down the stream, although the large bull-heads, which I used to try to catch as a small boy, had evidently deserted this stretch of the stream. We walked back to the jar, feeling considerably less buoyant than we had on setting off from home, and were very disappointed to find it still empty. In desperation we took the jar back to the bridge and caught a few shrimps – perhaps he would eat them.

It was just as well Fishy was responding to a cod diet because our initial attempts to get him back to normal food had failed miserably. Undaunted, however, we placed a pyrex dish filled with water inside a large cardboard box and surrounded the dish with a towel to make a clearly defined little pond. The freshwater shrimps and a little water weed were added, and we fixed a low perch by piercing the sides of the box and pushing a stick through. We made a polythene hood to cover the top of the box and placed Fishy in to test his reactions. To watch him, we made a further small hole in the side of the box so that, with the eye close to the hole, it was easy to see in, but from the inside the observer was unnoticed.

He sat beside his little pool with head cocked on one side, watching the freshwater shrimps skimming around among the weed, seeking a hiding place, but he stood aloof from such a miserable offering and made no attempt to enter the water at all. He appeared quite content and when we removed him at ten-fifteen pm for a feed he ate a record twelve pieces of cod, each about half an inch long and of pencil thickness. I placed each piece in his beak and then sat him on my arm so that he

54

could stretch his neck to swallow. At the end of this, the second full day, he had eaten four fish fingers.

I reported my abysmal failure at catching minnows to Mick, who suggested that I should try again in the river Cherwell. As I work near the river I went to a likely spot during the lunch break and placed the jar, neck facing downstream as directed, and left it to await my return after work. I could see straight away that there were no minnows in the jar despite the fact that several were swimming close by, so I dispensed with the screw top and in great triumph returned home and hour later with four extremely small fish. I had also retrieved from the river bed a small piece of tree root on which many little aquatic insects were crawling. I placed the contents in Fishy's dish and for the response I will quote from the daily log: 'Watched him through peep-hole in box – much bobbing and watching with head on side and then flew up on to perch. Soon after he plunged in several times and caught and swallowed something at least once. After several entries – sometimes standing in dish and probing at tree roots – he came out and preened thoroughly. Dish taken out and the two larger minnows eaten.'

This was good occupational therapy but it was certainly not going to satisfy his needs. The net widened. We scoured the local brooks and ponds, but apart from the occasional small minnow, the real quarry eluded us. Again I reported the lack of success to Mick and suggested that he should try his luck at minnow catching; after all it was he who had told me how easy it all was. The jar was duly returned to the original owner and he said, quite confidently, that he would call at my home shortly, with a plentiful supply. The week was slipping by and I knew it would be Sunday before he could bring them over, so our feeble attempts at catching sufficient to amuse him had to continue for another couple of days.

On Sunday morning I gave him his breakfast and assured him that Mick would be arriving a little later with the 'real thing'. I lacked confidence, however; how could anyone succeed where I had failed so miserably? After lunch, however, triumphantly carrying a bucket containing about eighty large minnows, Mick duly arrived. I could not wait to test Fishy's reaction and I took one minnow which had died in transit and offered it to him as he sat on his perch in the box. With a deft flick of the beak he aligned it head first and swallowed it without ceremony. Another one which had not survived the journey very well was dispatched similarly. What would he do with one of the more lively ones though? This question was soon answered when I managed to catch one which I held out for him. He grabbed it in his beak and proceeded to smash it against the perch until he was satisfied that it was dead and then he swallowed it with obvious relish.

He had eaten well through the day and therefore we did not offer any more fish but set about the task of keeping them alive until he required them for food. I was never very happy about feeding live fish; it seemed terribly barbaric keeping them alive for days on end just to end their lives bashed against Fishy's perch, but this would be happening if he were free, flying on his own stream, and it was no use becoming emotionally involved with minnows at this stage. We chose a discarded zinc washing tray for the minnows, placing them in the river water with a plentiful supply of water weed collected from the same source. They appeared quite happy in their new surroundings and Fishy was obviously delighted at his luxurious living. At ten-thirty pm that evening I placed a couple of minnows in Fishy's dish and he immediately dived in after one. He did not succeed in catching one but in the commotion one of them leapt out and I hand-fed it to him. The second one I also fed to him, and after a preen he was ready to settle for the night – so were we! When I peered in for a final check before going to bed I was thrilled to find that he had cast his first pellet, a mixture of cod skins and minnow bones measuring about an inch in length, cigar-shaped and about a quarter of an inch diameter at the centre. It was good to see this degree of normality returning to Fishy's life.

When we were in bed we talked for a long while about the

events of the past few days and laid plans for the next day. It was decided to obtain a larger box for Fishy, to give him more room to manoeuvre and allow space for a larger water dish. He had taken a few test flights in the room during the evening but we were convinced that it would be better for him to spend most of his time in the box. He always appeared to be either contemplating a fishing trip, catching fish, or preening and therefore he was not bored by his enforced captivity, nor did he attempt to escape. His new box was a grand affair measuring three feet by two feet by two feet six inches high, fitted with a couple of perches, a much larger pond, surrounded again by a towel, and the essential spy hole. He enjoyed the bigger home and spent a good deal of time flitting from perch to perch. When he was about to catch a fish he would bob excitedly and patter along the perch, head cocked, ready for the plunge.

His first attempts at fishing were not all successful by any means, however, and although he secured a large fish in his second dive in his new box, seven more abortive attempts followed during which he became *very* wet. We were concerned about him getting as wet as this and were relieved when he decided to preen himself thoroughly and dry out. The preening ritual was by now well established and carried out with meticulous precision. First a quick wipe over with the beak before preening left wing; right wing; breast; back; flanks and feet, in that order, finishing with a satisfied scratch of the head. It was interesting to note, later on, when he had achieved a well-oiled appearance, that a finale to the preening routine was often a quick rub of the wings against his flanks. This was carried out at a speed that was difficult to follow and reminded me of someone rubbing their hands together as one sometimes does when it is cold. The effect was similar too, because the friction caused by rubbing was often sufficient to raise steam from his wings!

The type of intimacy we were sharing with Fishy was different from anything we had experienced previously. We had shared the lives of many birds and the majority were prepared to accept our presence; in fact most of them sought our company when they were ill – old and young alike – but here was the opportunity to watch him whilst he was oblivious of our presence. He did not shun our company in the evenings but he showed obvious pleasure in the 'freedom' of his box.

His food supply was assured now and Mick spent the majority of his free time reverting to the occupation of his youth, catching at least thirty minnows a day which constituted Fishy's requirements. He cast a pellet each day; sometimes two, but they were extremely flimsy balls of delicate minnow bones and would disperse immediately if cast on to the water. I did manage to retrieve one or two and spray them with hair lacquer to hold them together but even these have disintegrated and the only one that I have to remind me of Fishy is the first one which is cemented together with cod skins.

We spent hours watching him from first light to bed-time and on several occasions we were privileged to see something which I have never seen repeated in the wild. He had depleted his supply of minnows in the dish one evening until only one small fish was left among the tangle of water weed. Several attempts had been made to secure the last elusive minnow without success, when he jumped into the water and deliberately shepherded the fish to one end of the dish. He then hooded his wings to form a complete canopy over his head and as the fish dived for cover he caught it with a nimble thrust. I can only assume that by holding his wings in this manner he was excluding the reflected light, thus giving himself a much clearer vision of the fish. Ironically, though, the fish, on each of the three occasions I witnessed this behaviour, swam under the hooded wings as if seeking shelter, thus sealing their fate. The behaviour, similar to that employed by certain herons, appeared completely natural and may be used in shallow water when fish are in short supply but, as I have said, I can find no record to substantiate this theory.

He spent seven days in his new box, coming out in the evening whilst I changed his water and towel and cleaned the perches. His flight was quite strong now and when he called, whilst lapping the room at incredible speed, the noise was ear-piercing. There was still one major obstacle to overcome before his final release and it was this that demanded our attention now, as we felt he should be ready to go before very long.

It had been interesting to watch his fishing techniques in shallow water but we knew that he would spend most of his time fishing from a perch over water, from which water he would have to become airborne again whilst carrying a fish. It was this ability we wished to test before being satisfied that he was truly ready to return to the wild. We had already decided that we would release him on the river which we now knew contained a plentiful supply of fish. Despite his daily demand, the fish were still arriving regularly and there were no obvious signs that the numbers were decreasing. We tried to induce him to fish from a perch placed over the zinc bath, but he only associated feeding with the time spent in his box and so some method had to be found to test his fishing skills in this new type of environment. We finally decided to obtain a really large, strong box and line the interior with polythene. This was a fairly simple matter because it was held in place at the bottom with a generous layer of washed gravel and secured at the top with strong staples. Water was added to a depth of about four inches (about four gallons of water) and into the gravel we planted water weed from the river. Above the water line we pierced the sides for his perches; one six inches, and one eight inches above the water and when we introduced twenty freshly caught minnows, the scene was set.

As soon as Fishy was introduced to his new quarters the minnows disappeared like quicksilver among the weeds, but he bobbed in obvious excitement and it was not long before he had plunged head long in. He did not catch a fish but the way in which he bobbed back on to his perch, eye immediately cocked for the next dive, gave us tremendous reassurance. Several times during the next few minutes he lunged in but failed to make a catch. He sat pensively for a while and then decided to preen thoroughly before making any further fishing dives. It was late in the evening and we feared that he might drown if left in this box all night, because if he attempted to enter the water in the dark, he might not regain his perch. It was very unlikely that such a mishap would occur but we were not taking any chances at this stage. He did not object to being resettled in his old box for the night and I went to bed, eagerly awaiting first light when I could give him his second chance in the grand arena.

I woke before it was light and had breakfasted when Fishy was ready to begin his day; normally about five-thirty am. I had to wait for a further twenty minutes before he was ready to take to the water and then he 'belly-flopped' in a couple of times (bathing dives) before commencing a particularly long and meticulous preen. I was anxious to observe a satisfactory conclusion to our experiment before I had to leave for work, but this was not to be and I left Joyce in charge, feeling rather deprived as I set off. He was obviously not feeling like an early breakfast and I wondered if my observations just after seven am were the reason. Again I quote from the log: '07.05: with head towards me (on near perch) he opened his beak wide and gaped and gave a few noiseless coughs as if to cast a pellet; then his head jerked peculiarly, like a ping-pong ball being bounced quickly about a quarter of an inch off the table. He then resettled. I'm sure it was connected with pellet casting although none came.' Was he waiting until the pellet had properly formed before beginning his day's fishing?

Joyce had to leave him for a while to go shopping and when she returned he was busily preening water from his feathers – still no proof! It was not until eleven-thirty that morning that he was observed actually catching a fish in his new box, and we had to wait until twelve-twenty before he tried again – this time he made two unsuccessful attempts in quick succession. By the afternoon he had conquered his new environment to the extent that he was making a catch at each second or third attempt. He never allowed himself to get too wet and spent much of his time preening.

I had wondered if he would tire when he really had to work for his fish, but in the evening, when a friend, Dr Bruce Campbell, called to see him, he had never looked better and he celebrated with five successful dives in quick succession, much to the amusement and astonishment of Bruce.

Unlike all the other birds I had cared for, he showed no significant change in his behaviour as he became fit and well, and although we were confident that he could be successfully released, we had hoped for positive signs on his part of his desire to go. Life was too good in the box now though for him to want to leave, and therefore the decision was left entirely to us. Both Fishy and I had had a long day when we finally retired for the night and I have no doubt that he was soon fast asleep. I could not settle so readily, and inwardly worried about his future. If we let him go too soon he would become weak again and die. If we delayed the release, he might become affected psychologically.

The next day I wondered why I had been so stupid. Fishy was ready to go and he soon made it obvious. He was still content to catch the fish that we placed so conveniently under his nose but he was restless, flying from perch to perch and looking up at the light overhead. A couple of times he flew at the polythene sheet which covered the top of the box in a clear indication that life had been good to him recently but that he wanted the wide open spaces. As soon as I arrived home from work in the afternoon, I telephoned Mick to tell him that I would be bringing Fishy to the minnows instead of the usual reverse procedure. He was anxious to witness the release, and within half an hour we had met beside the river where Fishy was to gain his freedom. It was a wonderful spot near an old mill where canal, river, mill-race and mill-pond formed a complex of fishing waters fit even for our bird.

I carried the box to the river bank and removed the polythene hood. Fishy sat sparkling in the glorious sunshine, looking around him to gain his bearings. Quite suddenly he was on the wing; across the river, up over a group of thorn bushes on the far side; a quick call and he was out of sight. He had arrived almost dead, and as I watched him leave, bubbling and effervescing with life, I felt the thrill that only such an occasion can give. We sat and chatted for a while in the warm sunshine, watching the minnows darting in the water, but we did not see him again and in any case he was on his own now.

We are tortured today with a feeling of intense guilt by the deeds committed by man against nature; hardly ever can we view a scene as nature intended. My early interest was sparked off by a close association with the truly wild things around me. I can remember watching a green woodpecker probing for ants in an old meadow near my home and becoming so absorbed that I imagined I was part of the invaded colony, marshalling forces against this huge adversary. Everywhere I looked, I could enter a tiny, natural world, where man played no part in the everyday lives of the inhabitants. These experiences can still be found, but ruthlessly and relentlessly their scenes are being taken for man's selfish needs. When, therefore, I share the thrill of its release to freedom with a bird which has spent some part of its life with me, I feel that I am, in some miserable way, avenging the injustice experienced by the wild creatures around me. It can be argued that it is unnatural to care for a sick animal; that they should die as nature intended, but many of the birds which come into my life are victims of road accidents and therefore the need to cure is even greater. I rarely stop to moralize or theorize about the causes which bring birds to me; they give me little time for this rather irrelevant exercise. But as I sat by the river, beside the box which until a few moments ago contained a perfect living creature about which my entire life had temporarily revolved, I felt very close to nature and extremely humbled by the experience.

6

Olly I

The problems and difficulties encountered whilst caring for sick or injured birds are far too numerous to catalogue, but basically they fall into two categories: the technical problems of producing an environment suitable for a kingfisher for example, or immobilizing a wing and building up a frame-work to secure the bone structure in place in order that the wing can properly heal; and the non-technical problem of interpreting the behaviour of a bird correctly in order to do what is necessary at the right time.

The latter of these two categories is by far the most difficult to come to grips with, mainly, I think, because it is almost impossible to acquire a bird's mind and fully understand what motivates any particular activity. Certainly hunger will promote food-begging calls from young birds if they see the possibility of food at hand. This we can appreciate, because we share the same need for food. Exhaustion will lead to sleep, for the same reason that we go to bed each night but here the human/bird analogy ends and the problem of understanding begins. A bird can certainly be content, perhaps even happy, but it has no way of indicating happiness; it can be alarmed, and has positive ways of showing this; but many of the subtle moods which we can express are either not shared by birds or not obviously displayed.

In full health a bird must remain alert to possible danger; it must, by patience or persistence, secure its food; sleep and keep its plumage in good condition. These are the main factors which occupy the lives of birds and in this way, uncluttered by the multitudinous demands upon our own minds, the motives which produce their behavioural patterns must be comparatively simple. If four basically simple motives occupy a major proportion of a bird's life, it is not hard to appreciate that set patterns soon become deeply established which in turn gives rise to immeasurable problems in captivity. In the adult, these fixed rules have to be overcome if it is to rest contentedly, feed and regain strength; but with a juvenile, cut off from its parents who would generally indicate the most suitable pattern of behaviour, the responsibility placed upon the foster-parents is enormous. The process of returning a young bird to the wild can be a long one, as with the case of the magpie, or Fred the starling, but unless one lives in an environment similar to the one in which the youngster is ultimately to be released, then the 'gradual' approach is not practical. This last point was brought home very forcibly by Olly, the young tawny owl, who spent a little over two months with us and probably taught us more about birds than any other single visitor we had kept before.

Olly was quite a character in every sense of the word, and I can only assume that he must have given his parents some uneasy moments before I met him because at least a week before he was due to leave the nest he was found sitting in the middle of a busy road. It was late at night and, assuming that the parents would be at hand, he was placed on the grass verge near to the hedge – he immediately shuffled into the road again. A second bid was made to thwart his suicide attempt by placing him actually on the hedge from which he could call to his parents: again abysmal failure, for he flopped on to the grass and made for the road. Nothing would dissuade him from making a bee-line for the road, and in the end he was brought to me to raise. He arrived, a bundle of grey, downy feathers from which emerged two very large, mischievous eyes. It was the evening of 13 May, 1971, and I wondered if it would prove lucky or unlucky.

He was plump and well-fed but I felt sure that the parents would normally have given him food during the night, so we gave him a few small pieces of liver which he accepted quite

64

readily once they had been placed in his beak, and then settled him in a box for the night. The night was to be a short one for me because by now it was well past midnight and at about five-thirty am I was awoken by the most fearful squabble between rival male blackbirds on the lawn beneath our bedroom window. I looked out to see what all the fuss was about and saw two birds locked in combat, feathers flying and feet flailing, shouting abuse at each other. Eventually one of them struggled free and fled over the wall into the field beyond, whilst the other straightened out what feathers he had left and flew into a tree to pronounce his victory. The incident in itself was not terribly significant but I saw in the bundle of feathers on the lawn, sufficient roughage to last a young tawny owl all day.

I had gone to sleep pondering the problem of feeding Olly, and already I was half-way towards a decent meal. Half a dozen pieces of liver rolled in blackbird's feathers were received very gratefully and I was extremely relieved by his ready response to food. During the day everything went well and in the evening I gave him a strip of beef which he held in his talons while attempting to tear pieces off with his beak. I thought this was a clear indication that his parents had ceased to feed titbits and were at least encouraging the young to prepare the meals themselves.

Satisfied that he had settled into his new environment sufficiently to feed well, my attention turned to accommodation. Was the cardboard box adequate, or could he become bored without company or sight of the outside world? By now I had acquired a comprehensive collection of boxes, baskets, cages and other paraphernalia, and I decided to fit out a wire-fronted box, which measured about two feet long by fifteen inches high and wide with a log to perch on, a water dish and some pieces of rotting wood with which to amuse himself between feeds and periods of sleep. He sat snugly on Joyce's lap whilst I attended to his new home and when I placed him inside he appeared to enjoy exploring his new surroundings. After a complete inspection he lay down (looking more like a kitten than an owl) and went to sleep. I was very relieved that many potential problems had not materialized, but I could not help feeling that success was still a long way off and Joyce and I sat down to plan the future.

Parent birds have two main advantages over the human foster; they instinctively know what food to give to the young (albeit they work extremely hard to acquire sufficient supply) and, equally important, they appear to share little or none of the emotional strain concerning the welfare of the young. Instinct drives them on to do everything possible to ensure the survival of their offspring, but if things just do not work out, they can abandon the attempt without concern. This is certainly not my experience and I find, all too often, that I am either beside myself with anxiety because progress is not being maintained at the expected level or, fearing complacency, I try to predict future problems which I convince myself will occur. This type of tension often inhibits the establishment of a genuine relationship with birds, but it is difficult if not impossible to overcome.

Any problems which we might have predicted did not materialize for the first couple of days, however, and Olly continued to eat well, sleep contentedly and sit comfortably on Joyce's lap for an hour in the evening. We tried hard to vary his diet and included liver, mutton and beef mixed with sheep's wool or feathers for roughage; small earthworms; mealworms and pulped birds which we had retrieved from the roadside. We found the latter a very useful source of food, and although hammering unfortunate accident victims such as blackbirds, thrushes, rabbits and any other 'natural' food is a grisly business, we steeled ourselves to do it feeling sure that no substitute could be fully adequate.

Sheer inquisitiveness as to what lay beyond his immediate surroundings had led to his initial problems, and I am quite sure that the same reason led to our first crisis on the third morning of his stay with us. I dragged myself, rather unwillingly, from bed at about five-thirty am to ensure that all was well and was immediately filled with horror as I looked into his cage. His beak and breast feathers were covered in blood, and fresh blood was trickling slowly but persistently from an open wound just above the upper mandible. The cause was soon obvious; a small piece of wire was protruding beyond the wooden batten which fixed it to the front of the cage, and in his constant search for a way out during the night to explore the room beyond, he had chafed a nasty wound. I called to Joyce and we tried to clean him up to assess the actual damage. As is often the case, the situation at first appeared far worse than it really was and with the blood removed and a patch of soft tissue placed over the beak to stem the bleeding (my usual cure for a nick whilst shaving) he looked much better. To be truthful, he did not appear very concerned in the first place but lack of concern in the face of grave personal injury appeared to be his hallmark and we were left wondering what form the next crisis would take. There was a real lesson to be learned, however, and ever since I have been very suspicious of any sharp obstacles associated with bird-cages. Our relief did not end here, however, for when I removed the blood-stained newspaper from the floor of the cage I found a sizeable pellet with a blood clot on one end – was this a result of internal injury or was it, as we hoped, connected with the beak injury? We could only wait to find this out; another addition to the list of tension factors.

During the day Joyce fed him nine times at about two-hourly intervals and, although his intake of food varied on each occasion, he took in total sixty-three pieces of meat, each about the size of a hazel nut. The day's supply consisted of pulped mistle thrush, pieces of liver, and beef cut from the lower jaw with the skin and hair intact. Eight or nine pieces of meat, I reckoned, would be equivalent to a good-sized mouse and by nightfall I was satisfied that any young owl which had consumed seven mice during the day should survive without nutritional problems. At bed time we decided that, although freedom to explore the room unhindered would almost certainly land our new acquisition in some sort of trouble, it was preferable to a fresh bout of beak-chafing, and therefore the wire front was removed from the cage and it was placed on the floor with some food and water near the open door. Furniture was moved away from the walls so that he could ɪ ot become trapped behind it and all small objects were removed from the shelves and cupboard tops in an effort to avoid calamity. When I ventured into the room the next morning I was pleased to find him contentedly sleeping on a pile of torn-up toilet tissues near to the cage, and although I could trace his movements all around the room from the sequence of droppings, both the furniture and the owl had come through the night unscathed.

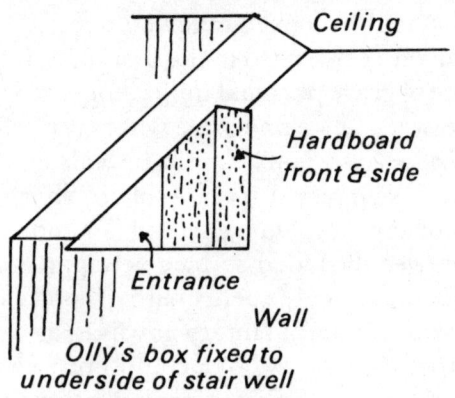

For the next ten days life was rather quiet; Joyce still fed him regularly, although food was left for him during the night, and gradually he was being weaned off hand-feeding. He thoroughly enjoyed a couple of hours each evening in our company when he would sit on Joyce's lap pecking at her skirt or making sallies on to her shoulder to inspect her hair. Fluffy grey down was being replaced by handsome tawny feathers and, to respect his natural instinct to be active by night and sleep during the day, I constructed a retreat for him beneath the stairs (see sketch). This worked like a charm. He could secure privacy whenever he chose and right from the start he rarely ventured out before the children were safely in bed and life at home took on a less hectic pace. Each evening, at about nine pm, he would come to the front of the box and examine the room in detail, appearing anxious if Joyce was not in her usual place on the settee to talk to him and spend half an hour or so enjoying each other's company. The evening's activity soon became a ritual, beginning with some 'small talk' as he sat on her shoulder, followed by meticulous preening of the hairs on her neck after which he reached round, straining on tiptoes, to preen her eyebrows and eyelashes. Quite what the significance of the exercise was I do not know, but it appeared very important to Olly and he would not settle to anything else until this had been properly and thoroughly achieved.

When he had satisfied himself that my wife's plumage was in good shape he would then search for the toilet roll (a necessity in any room which contains a well-fed owl). There were few places to hide anything in this room as most articles had been removed to avoid breakages or were considered potentially dangerous to an inquisitive owl, and therefore a cursory glance round with his all-seeing eyes would soon locate the quarry. It was amusing to watch him prepare to pounce on the unsuspecting toilet roll. He would elongate his body, revealing extraordinarily long legs, and at the same time rotate his head excitedly. He would then break into a little dance, shifting the weight from one leg to the other as if in response to some distant war drums. Finally, he would thrust his body forward and pounce – talons forward and wings flapping over the victim. The wing flapping was obviously used to maintain balance on a rather unstable object, but I have since watched other owls 'strike' and I think the wings are used only partially to maintain balance and are also employed to maintain a weightless condition, thus allowing freer movement of the feet. They also add the benefit of completely baffling the victim.

This type of play was obviously necessary to acquire the right co-ordination of eyes and limbs and we were delighted one evening when, tiring of the toilet roll, he pounced on a fluffy little toy panda which belonged to my son, Alan. We allowed him to play for some time and then took it from him and threw it on to the floor a few feet away. He watched intently, waiting for it to move, and then finally struck at it with obvious mock aggression. I immediately realized that we had made a positive breakthrough; with the panda we could teach him many tricks of the trade which one day would earn him his livelihood. Alan saw the situation in a different light however and it was difficult to persuade him that his panda was being sacrificed in a good cause.

Following a session of play, which could last until about ten pm, he would normally take a good feed and at this stage (we had had him just over a fortnight) he followed this by a period of throat-flapping. With beak wide open, and his body elongated vertically, his throat would flap, rather in the same manner as a dog will pant. I have often wondered about the true cause of this behaviour because, although it is known to be associated with an over-heated condition, it is often practised just after a meal and in conjunction with wide gaping, as if trying unsuccessfully to cast a pellet. Whether it has anything to do with the recent intake of food, however, I have never really established.

I was extremely pleased with Olly's progress to date but unfortunately we could spend only a brief period together in the evening. He would be preparing for an active night whilst I was anxious to get some rest and, despite my desire to watch him as much as possible, I usually retired about midnight, leaving him to play with his panda and do whatever else he did during the night. Each morning I would find a fresh pellet in his cage, which varied enormously in size from small ones no larger than a pea, to one quite huge pellet which contained the head and wings of a blackbird, measured no less than five inches long and resembled the shape of a scythe blade.

I was missing a great deal by going to bed and that was remedied when I developed an extremely painful whitlow on my finger. For about four nights, sleep was out of the question and therefore I sat in subdued light to examine Olly's nocturnal behaviour. Quite what I had expected to see I do not know, but I had almost dozed off out of sheer exhaustion before there was any sign of activity at all. He had been sitting on the bookcase, occasionally preening, when I was alerted by a sudden movement: he stiffened and shuffled to the edge to look over and began his little dance. Obviously something had attracted his attention. His eyes were riveted to a spot near the table leg but I could see nothing in the dim light. The dance continued and his head rotated excitedly. I peered closer and could just about make out the shape of a small woodlouse which had obviously made its way in under the front door, I could not help feeling that in doing so it had made a serious mistake. I could recognize all the signs of an imminent pounce and I was quite sure that Olly would drop on to the woodlouse in the same way he had done so many times on to the panda. This, however, was my mistake, because when he descended he landed about two feet away from the insect and from there continued his dance until he had worked himself into a positive frenzy. He then ran forward on ridiculously long legs (I described him in my notes taken at the time as ostrich-like) and proceeded to dance around the insect with wings held out, rather like the courtship dance of a crane. I was very surprised by this quite unexpected behaviour and I was not alone. No matter which way the little woodlouse turned, he was confronted by a frenzied owl. I waited with bated breath for the final assault on the victim but unnoticed by me, and presumably by Olly, the woodlouse had gradually made ground towards the bookcase and, when he finally disappeared beneath, it left four eyes focused on the exit, all displaying sheer disbelief at the result.

After I had collected my thoughts, I wondered how often this had occurred. Had I witnessed his first encounter with live prey? This would at least explain his failure to make a kill. Or was he perfecting some technique which would some day see the downfall of his future rodent victims? So many unanswered questions from one small observation, and I was very intrigued and impatient for the next nocturnal prowler to enter the arena. If the owl still had a great deal to learn, then so had the woodlouse, because not many minutes elapsed before he was in open country again, this time making a bee-line for the door. He could have chosen to stay put, or creep unnoticed around the edge of the room, but instead he trundled straight across the floor. Olly was into his dance again in a flash and some of the original excitement still remained. He pranced and stepped around the woodlouse, maintaining an absolute fix on him with his eyes despite his wild body movements, but this time the woodlouse kept going. The encircling steps gradually closed until Olly was describing a circle of no more than six inches in diameter around it, but even then the woodlouse made the sanctuary offered by my armchair before the owl had taken any decisive action. I had felt that this time I was about to witness his first kill and I am sure we both experienced a feeling of extreme anticlimax.

I sat for a long while afterwards trying to understand how someone like myself, so opposed to indiscriminate killing, could become so tense and excited by the cavorting of an owl around a poor little creature like a woodlouse. Tense and excited I had been, however, and I had lived through an experience quite new to me. As to the rest of the night, I have little recollection because I felt extremely tired and, despite the pain from my finger, I could not force myself to take any more notes. When Joyce appeared on the scene in the morning I recounted my experiences and I felt that I now knew a little more about a tawny owl.

I had to visit the doctor during the day to arrange for treatment at the local hospital for my finger and in the afternoon I gained some much-needed rest. As Olly prepared himself for another night of activity, I found myself excited at the prospect of joining him, rather than going to bed in the usual manner. As before, the early part of the evening passed without event until, about one o'clock in the morning, an earwig breezed in under the door. One thing was certain, more visitors entered the house via the front door than either myself or Joyce had ever suspected! Although Olly was some ten feet from the door at the time, sitting nonchalantly on the mantle shelf, he spotted the intruder instantly and broke into his war dance. I had a job to follow the progress of the earwig across the floor but by his fixed stare, I could tell that Olly was not sharing my problem. He had barely achieved full tempo when he lunged from the shelf and to my surprise, landed right on the earwig and actually clutched it in his talons. He passed it to his beak very nimbly and ate it with the same relish and speed as he used to dispose of hand-fed mealworms. Why, when he could land so accurately on an earwig, had he danced around the woodlouse? Was it suspicion of the first – did he see in the earwig a more instantly recognizable meal? I do not know; I can only say that when a beetle entered the room just before dawn, he compromised between his original performance with the woodlouse and his more positive encounter with the earwig. This time he landed about six inches away and scurried after the beetle, catching it with his beak and eating it with a series of audible crunches. One thing was obvious, he was gaining experience in the skills he would require in the wild and I felt extremely satisfied with my nocturnal observations. I smiled as I imagined him hunting beetles in the grass and among the stones where the game of hide and seek (played for real) would be much more exacting and obviously would require much dancing, prancing and chasing; occupations not always associated with owls.

Olly was growing up and although he still retained the baby fluff on top of his head and lacked the beautiful dark streaks on his breast, his general appearance was much more adult. He spent many hours preening his newly gained feathers and I wondered if he felt the same pride as I did when I acquired my first suit with long trousers. It was about this time he took his first bath. We made sure that he always had drinking water available and we used a shallow glass dish for the purpose. Joyce called to me one evening, stating that Olly was trying to bathe in his water dish. It was amusing to see a fully grown owl sitting in a dish no larger than a saucer and thrashing his wings with little or no effect. The movements were quite instinctive

73

but the result was most unsatisfactory and so we quickly fetched a shallow metal tray about eighteen inches square and poured water in to a depth of about an inch. As soon as Joyce splashed the water with her finger he seized the opportunity of a real bath. The mess which followed was unbelievable but when he emerged with plus-fours tight against his legs and wet, spiky feathers sticking out from his chin to his trouser tops, we could not choke a smile. For Olly it was a very serious business though and he flew up on to the television set to shake and preen himself back to his more usual splendour. After that he enjoyed a bath daily and invariably flew on to the television to complete his toiletry.

His favourite perching places were always covered with newspaper but in the case of the television I cut a piece of plywood to fit over the top in order to avoid damage to the cabinet and, more importantly, to stop any droppings from going down the back and into the works. This appeared to work well and soon he almost abandoned his box in favour of the television as a day-time roost. All went well until one evening a friend who had spent a couple of hours with us decided to leave. It was just on ten o'clock and I switched the television on to watch the national news. Olly had been rather quiet, waiting for the visitor to leave before beginning his evening's activities, and he took his cue to come to life when John reached the door. He shuffled to the back of the television and 'raised his tail' – nothing very unusual about that but someone had moved the plywood forward a couple of inches. A white splodge landed plumb on target and blue sparks, accompanied by a cloud of steam erupted from the television whilst the picture degenerated into a bright spot on the screen before I could reach the switch to put the set off. My friend was absolutely amazed and even Olly peered over to see why the picture had disappeared. I was reluctant to switch on again later to see if the television would work, but it was soon clear that something major had gone wrong inside. I called for the engineer the next day who came out to repair the set whilst I was at work. He explained to

Joyce that the condenser was at fault but that in all of his experience he had never encountered a case before where the faulty part was covered in a powdery white substance. He could offer no explanation but fortunately did not expect a mere female to be able to explain such a peculiar phenomenon.

Days and weeks slipped by and the toy panda became a mangled heap of rags and fluff under the constant attention of Olly. To make him even more sharp and accurate we used to make a mock mouse which we tied to a piece of string and snatched it around on the floor. He would watch from the television perch and suddenly pounce, gripping it firmly in his talons and squeaking harshly if we tried to take it away.

Watching a baby grow and blossom forth into maturity is a wonderful experience; full of surprises, disappointments, moments of pride and pleasure, in fact a complete range of emotions associated with the close contact between interdependent beings. I say interdependent because the helpless baby, whether human child or bird, is very much at the mercy of the parent (or foster, in the case of 'our' birds) and we, in turn, are dependent upon the birds for information they can relate to us regarding their requirements. Always awaiting the subtle clues which will tell us how we should react, produces a bond which is difficult to describe.

One early morning, at about five am, when Olly had been with us for about five weeks, I came down stairs and was immediately filled with horror. He was lying completely prostrate on the floor with wings and tail spread out like a huge fan around him. I had become accustomed to his soft 'hoot' of recognition as I entered the room but there was no sound or movement; he lay completely still. I spoke to him without response and even when I touched him there was no sign of life at all. I called frantically to Joyce who came rushing down in a state of near-panic. When I knelt beside him, I could just make out the rise and fall of his feathers which indicated that he was breathing but he was obviously in some state of coma. Joyce also knelt beside him and we sought for an explanation – had he, in some mysterious way, broken his legs and finally dragged himself into this grotesque position before losing consciousness through exhaustion? Could he possibly have had a bone stuck in his throat and struggled frenziedly to dislodge it? None of the possibilities appeared likely, but there he lay, more helpless than the first day we had set eyes on him.

Finally he blinked, muttered softly under his breath in a tone we associated with annoyance, and stiffly shuffled a couple of feet out of the shadow Joyce was casting over him as she obstructed the early morning rays of sun shining through the window, and took up his original pose again. Sunbathing! We felt suddenly relieved and also embarrassed by our unnecessary concern. I had watched tawny owls many times in the wild but I had certainly never seen anything like that. To Olly's annoyance we put it to the test again, Joyce moving to place him in her shadow once more. This time he reacted more swiftly and swore more loudly and so we left him until the natural movement of the sun's rays terminated his pleasure and under protest, he retreated to his day-time roost on the television. I was greatly intrigued by the whole performance. Not only was it something completely unexpected and new to me, I could not help thinking that if Olly, or owls in general, allowed themselves to plunge into blissful coma like this each sunny morning, they would be extremely vulnerable to attack by predators.

The next morning I again woke early and went to see if he would repeat the operation. I was greeted by a complete circle of feathers on the floor: his wings were thrust forward, like the arms of a diver entering the water, and his fanned tail completed the arc. It was an incredible sight and again he appeared in a state of hypnotic ecstasy. I witnessed this behaviour on three separate occasions but, true to form, we were rather short of sunny mornings for the rest of his stay and therefore it was impossible to test the regularity of this peculiar ritual. I can only say that since this time I have had ample opportunity to watch another tawny owl which was raised in a very similar manner but which has never, to my knowledge indulged to the

76

same extent in the unconscious bliss of sunbathing. Olly II certainly enjoys sitting in the sun but is prepared to settle for what appears a much more natural occupation.

The time spent with Olly had taught us a great deal, but our thoughts turned towards the eventual release. He had proved to us that he could recognize and deal with natural prey and, although still very affectionate, his mock attacks at my son's bare feet, a common practice in the mornings, began to have more meaning. Sometimes he would positively shun our company and we felt that he was ready to take up his true place in life.

Once again the tormenting questions of where and when welled up in our thoughts. A pair of tawny owls frequent the farm and fields adjoining our garden and therefore it seemed sensible to release him in a more suitable area away from home.

Eventually plans were laid and we decided, with permission from a friend, to release him in a private, wooded area, about a mile from my home. He had become very attached to his television roost and therefore to make the break as easy as possible for him, we fixed an old television cabinet in a large yew tree. The cabinet had been completely stripped and in it we placed water, a dish of food and a few pieces of rotten wood which he enjoyed pecking. About six-thirty pm, on the afternoon of 10 July, Joyce, my three children, Lynda, Mike and Alan, myself and Olly, set off for the wood. I placed the cardboard box in which I had carried him near the old television cabinet and, when I opened it, Olly immediately jumped into his new 'home'. He carefully inspected his surroundings and then came to the open front to look out upon his woodland territory. We waited expectantly for about a quarter of an hour but with the patience typical of an owl he just sat looking back at us. Quite what we had thought was going to happen I do not know but eventually we tore ourselves away and with a last round of good-byes we trudged rather sadly back through the woods.

That evening the house lacked life: no inquisitive eyes watching every movement from the television, no soft call or snap of the beak as we passed, no soft feathers against the cheek in the late evening – in short, no Olly, and we missed him very much. We were thrilled, naturally, that he had eventually taken up residence in the wild, but could he compete? We had planned to visit the wood each evening for the first week or two in order to place food in the box to supplement his diet if necessary. I thought about him a great deal during his first day of freedom and was anxious to pay him a visit in the hope that I could establish that all was well. The whole family shared my anxiety and joined me in the trip to the wood. As we approached my heart pounded. Present or absent? Dead or alive? Our pace quickened and our ears and eyes strained for a tell-tale movement or noise.

The box was empty; just as we had left it, with food and water intact. He had left shortly after us the evening before because there were no familiar white droppings in the box. We looked around in the nearby trees and bushes but there was no trace. At least we had the satisfaction that he had left his box voluntarily because there was no sign of feathers which we felt sure would have marked a struggle. I explained to my young son, Alan, that he had flown away to another part of the wood which he would enjoy better and inwardly hoped sincerely that I was right.

The ritual visit to the deserted television cabinet continued for a fortnight and at each visit the likelihood of ever seeing him again decreased. I had decided that there was no further value in visiting the site after such a long period but Alan, whose concern for Olly's welfare had never diminished, persuaded me to take him for one final check. It was a hot evening and the wood was humming with the sound of busy insects. I tried several times to make excuses to come back but each time Alan's objections drove me on. When we arrived at the yew tree I cast a casual glance at the empty box, lifted Alan up to satisfy himself that the box was, in fact, empty, and turned rather wearily for home. After we had walked for about twenty paces down the path Alan looked into a holly tree and said, 'There's Olly.' I was pleased that something had sufficiently resembled an owl to satisfy him that Olly was still in the wood and remarked how nice it was to see him again. I was, at the time, several yards in front of him and therefore I could not see into the tree myself. I urged Alan to follow me in case he suddenly realized that he was not looking at an owl at all, but he stood rooted to the spot and insisted that I should go back to look for myself. It soon became obvious that I had to retrace my steps if only to retrieve a very obstinate son, but my patience was wearing a little thin. As I approached the base of the tree a large brown bird glided silently down from one of the upper branches and soft feathers brushed my face as it passed by. Before I could recover from the shock, Olly was safely tucked away in another holly bush a few yards away, calling very softly to us. A couple of blackbirds had spotted him and set up an incessant chackle, soon to be joined by others. The total excitement was summed up in Alan's face. His eyes twinkled, partly with tears of joy, and we stood enjoying a few moments of sheer magic together. Moments like these are indescribable and they are to be fully savoured because they are very rarely repeated.

We returned home and poured forth the good news. Surely after a fortnight in the wild Olly was quite capable of fending for himself. We slept that night with very light hearts.

Having found his day-time roost, I felt sure that we could quite easily pay him the odd visit to maintain some sort of relationship but a few days later we established that he had moved on again. A further two months passed and despite fairly regular visits to the wood we had found no trace of him. We were not terribly concerned now, merely a little disappointed but there were other problems arriving at home which needed attention – Olly had no need of us now.

About the end of September I paid a brief visit to the wood with Joyce to release a couple of song-thrushes which had spent a few days with us and, as it was a pleasant evening, we decided to walk around the lake in preference to returning straight home. The pathway took us past a small stand of very old yew trees and quite suddenly and silently from one of the trees a tawny owl drifted towards us. He flew between us at head level, brushing our faces with his wing tips, before the resident starlings rushed in with a screaming assault. He was completely unperturbed by all the fuss and swept gracefully back up into the yew trees. The chackle of excited birds rang through the woods and the blood raced through our veins. I had no proof that this was Olly – we were about a third of a mile from the place where he had been liberated – but it was inconceivable that any other owl would have behaved in this manner. I was very surprised that he had broken cover to greet us after such a long parting but never had a greeting been so warmly received. I was sure that our brief encounter would be the last tangible contact with Olly but strangely, a year later, whilst walking alone in the wood one morning I heard a soft hoot as I passed under a large chestnut tree and once again he swept past, close enough for his feathers to brush my face. Why he felt it necessary to make physical contact on these occasions I do not know. Why had he not chosen the many other occasions when we must have passed close by? These are questions to which there are no answers; we were content with the thought that a small spark of recognition still remained in a truly wild bird.

Olly I and the author take a stroll in the garden

Royston the baby heron:
fed on raw fish mashed
with warm milk

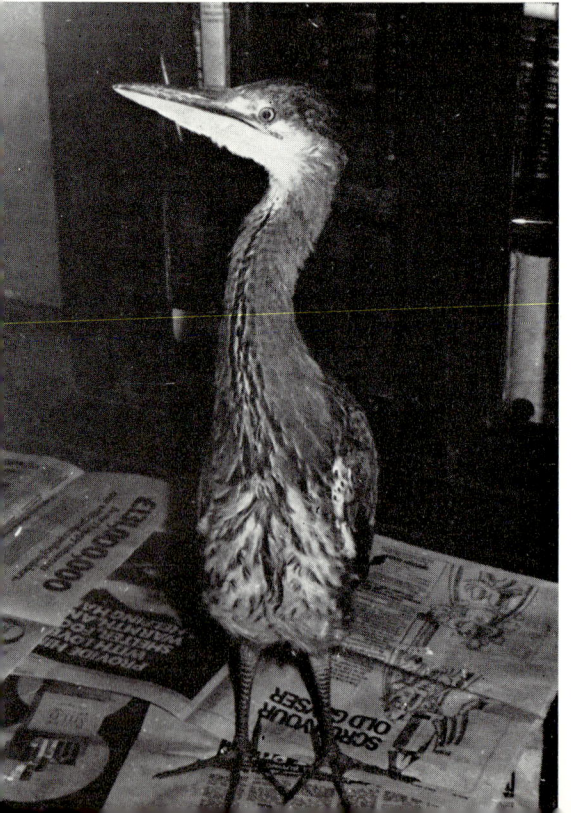

Not a bird to share a house
with: when grown, Royston
had a six-foot wing span
and a rapier-sharp beak

7

A problem from the tree-tops

Some birds move into the house almost unnoticed; some require a little modification to the lay-out in one of the rooms to suit their requirements; but until the arrival of Royston we had always managed to fit them in somewhere. But then Royston was so very different from any bird which we had previously encountered at home, and even the rather spacious accommodation offered by a rambling old stone house provided few design features compatible with the needs of a heron.

Everything about these magnificent birds requires space: enough room to exercise a six-foot wing span; a good area to stalk around on incredibly large feet, and, equally important, the opportunity for a mere human to manoeuvre out of range of a rapier-like beak.

The first hint of the problems we were to encounter came when a close friend of mine telephoned me at work to say that he had just deposited a young heron with my wife and suggested that I should apply some immediate thought to the matter before calling Joyce with initial instructions. I plied him with questions to try to establish a clear picture of the situation, and soon learned that on a routine visit to the heronry near his home he had found a very weak and cold youngster on the woodland floor beneath one of the nests. It is a well-established fact that any young heron which has the misfortune to fall from the nest (in this case situated about eighty feet up among the tree-tops) is abandoned by the parents, mainly, one must assume, because of the very real problems the birds would experience in trying to manoeuvre in the lower, dense cover.

There was no alternative but to rescue the pathetic little creature and try to foster it until it was ready to face the world on its own.

Royston (the friend) had one thought in mind; to get to my house before the little heron died and he made the twelve-mile dash in his car in record time. He did delay sufficiently long to call at his own house to raid the fridge and bring with him the family's supper, a quantity of fish; and he had collected some twigs in order to make a typical nest in the bottom of a large cardboard box. Joyce realized that warmth was the prime ingredient for immediate survival and cradled the ungainly youngster in her lap with her hands cupped over his back. He was about as big as a moorhen with enormous feet and a three-inch long bill, totally out of proportion for his size. The feathers on his head were coated with partly digested fish, collected presumably by thrusting his head down his parent's throat for food. At first he was very nervous, his body quivering from fear and cold, but he soon settled as the warmth penetrated his body and he fell into an exhausted sleep.

The discussion on the telephone with Joyce had been brief because she was anxious to warm him and avoid further complications from exposure, but we had decided to try to feed him a mash made from raw fish and warm milk. She would try to place a little in his beak to test his reaction and then, hopefully, feed him the rest from her cupped hand. We considered that a mixture of this nature, taken from a partially clasped hand, was as near to the real thing as possible.

He had arrived at eleven-thirty am, on 19 May, 1973, and by midday Joyce considered that he was ready for his first feed. How he would react to fish fingers, of course, was quite another matter. It proved to be no mean task to open his beak one-handed whilst trying to place a fish mash in it with the other, but in this way she managed to induce him to take about a quarter of a fish finger and an hour later she repeated the dose. After a further hour's rest he finished off the first fish finger and then, with every sign of contentment, he tucked in his head and slept soundly on her lap for two hours.

When he awoke at four pm he appeared much more confident in his new surroundings and took half a fish finger with considerable relish. Joyce was surprised when the little ungainly youngster stretched, scratched and proceeded carefully to preen his feathers. In common with most birds, pedicure formed an important part of the 'clean up' routine and he carefully inspected each huge toe in turn, removing all foreign matter before sitting back on his haunches with an air of sublime contentment. He was a smart little fellow now, fluffed and warm with the black tips of his wing feathers just emerging from steel blue quills. The peach-coloured shoulder patch contrasted beautifully with the various shades of grey which formed his general colouring, added to by the white chin and ear patch, yellow lower mandible and black streaks on his breast.

The early stages of recovery were achieved without problem and Joyce was both relieved and encouraged. It is always much easier to apply thought to a problem when the mind is free from worry, and when I returned home at six pm Joyce had already administered yet another feed and, although I had to face the prospect of getting my own tea, the heron was resting peacefully; warm, well-fed and happy. He remained in this blissful state for a further hour before surprising my wife yet again. He rose slowly and deliberately on uncertain legs, excreted a vast amount of white fluid over the edge of the 'nest' and proceeded to cackle loudly for food. The call notes were new to us, individual young being indistinguishable amid the cacophony of sounds in the heronry, but it can best be described phonetically as 'cack, cack, cack, cack, cack' often repeated with deliberation for long periods at a time. The call notes and general gesturing prior to a feed took on a new significance later during his stay with us.

Joyce answered his call with another large feed of fish mash, and this time he pecked at the remains of the feed from her hand

– this was progress indeed and, from that point on, he took food regularly from a saucer with no encouragement from either of us.

That evening some very good friends of ours came, partly, I think, to see us, but mainly to see the new arrival and take some photographs. We try to keep a photographic record of the birds when this is practical, but of course many of the more interesting shots are missing for the want of a camera at the right time or, more often, because the birds have been camera-shy and we have not felt justified in causing any more anxiety than absolutely necessary. Photographs of fully co-operative subjects are a source of great joy to us, but a cowering beast on film in these circumstances can do nothing but embarrass the photographer.

Royston, however, appeared ready for anything now and did not object in the slightest when transferred to Margaret's lap whilst Joyce, Trevor and I made preparations for his stay. The large cardboard box offered sufficient space for immediate requirements but the initial suggestion of a twig nest in the bottom seemed harsh treatment for an unbrooded youngster and therefore we compromised by covering the nest with a woollen jumper.

Before we put the newly prepared home to the test we decided to take some photographs. The towel on Margaret's lap and her white jumper formed an ideal background and therefore there was no need for further preparation. Olly II often had his photograph taken whilst similarly placed and paid no attention at all and there was no reason to suspect that Royston would object. In fact, I think it would be incorrect to state that he did object, but when the flash fired he literally jumped with quite a violent reaction. I am sure that there is a perfectly sound reason why some birds appear to ignore flash, whilst others are startled, but I have noticed that birds with yellow eyes like herons and little owls, for instance, show considerable reaction whilst the large, black-eyed birds like tawny owls and lapwings appear not to notice a flash at all. Herons' eyes are angled in the head so that they look down the long bill with the accuracy of a hunter sighting along the barrel of a rifle and, although they are not equipped to see in very poor light, they miss nothing during daylight hours, especially an electronic flash.

He was none the worse for his ordeal, however, and contented himself with pecking at the towel and occasionally preening. During preening, an oily substance was exuded from his nostrils and dispersed over the feathers and although this gave him a distinctly fishy smell, he looked extremely smart and well dressed. How the oil was produced, and where it came from, I was never sure.

Bed-time arrived with the usual apprehension for the night ahead, but he settled into his box willingly and I set the alarm for three am so that I could check to make sure that all was well. He had eaten six fish fingers during the first twelve hours with us and I had no real concern for him for a few hours. I was in a deep sleep when the alarm clock roused me and I staggered downstairs, blinking in the harsh light. Royston was equally sound asleep but, when I laid my hand on him to ensure that he was warm enough, a bright eye opened and he snapped into action. He rose on rather wobbly legs and 'chackled' excitedly. The silence of the night was shattered and Olly II, who had been watching from his perch on the television, blinked and stared in disapproval. Royston's tummy gave forth an enormous rumble and suddenly the corner of the box was awash with fluid white excreta. Quite naturally, none of our birds are house-trained but this little fellow was presenting a problem hitherto never experienced. I placed a large quantity of absorbent tissue in the corner of the box but I realized that maintaining hygiene, so essential when caring for any animals, was going to be a fearful task.

Having woken, he demanded food, and quickly consumed a fish finger. Morning might have dawned a little early but he was certainly ready for it, being galvanized into action from the moment his eyes opened. He insisted on preening and I felt obliged to allow this for I certainly did not want him to learn idle habits from me. After about three-quarters of an hour he seemed ready to settle again, so I covered the box as a precaution against Olly, put out the light and retreated to the sanctuary of my own bed. I lay there for some time recalling the hours spent with our new guest and finally fell asleep whilst listening to the garden robin singing his first few notes. His nest contained four young and was placed in a hole in the boundary wall of the garden, and I remember hoping that nothing would go wrong there to necessitate any further fostering whilst the heron was with us.

At breakfast-time he was ready to greet the day again with renewed vigour and, although the first few hours had been spent satisfactorily, two problems remained. The first, and most pressing, regarded his living accommodation and we decided that until he was old enough to be housed in the shed outside, we would just have to maintain a constant supply of large boxes and discard them frequently. This was not difficult because I could easily bring home as many as I wanted from the shop: obtaining a constant supply of fish, however, was going to prove very expensive. In any case, herons will eat a wide variety of food including frogs, small birds, mice and rats, and we were keen to supply a more interesting diet. At the same time we were uncertain as to when these variations of diet should be introduced.

Some of the adult herons were returning to the nest with fish in their beaks; they could be seen flying over my friend's house from their foraging trips to the river Cherwell, so we felt happy that he could accept food which had not been predigested, but how would he get on with feathers, fur, etcetera? We knew that owls needed roughage from an early age and strongly suspected that a heron's requirements would be similar, but the pellets found under the nest were consistently large, suggesting that they had all come from adult birds. Unlike those of birds of prey, however, they varied enormously in size and it was impossible to draw any conclusions. We would have to experiment carefully and hope that we were doing the right thing.

The opportunity came almost immediately when, on my way to work, I found a recently-killed rabbit beside the road. The lunch-time report from my wife was very encouraging; Royston had already eaten five fish fingers mashed with milk, and to one of these feeds she had added ten spots of cod liver oil. We were naturally anxious to try out the new food and we were pleased when he readily took four pieces of rabbit about the size of a walnut and even more pleased when, half an hour later, he took nineteen fair-sized portions!

He demanded, and got, a tremendous amount of attention and settled down very quickly. Most birds are initially suspicious of our two dogs, a golden labrador and a big fluffy keeshond, although the dogs themselves have learned to ignore birds; but Royston just looked them over with interest and then ignored them. Olly II, whom I have mentioned before, is a long-stay tawny owl with a crooked left leg and, although we have to isolate the small birds from him, we felt sure that Royston and he would be all right as long as we were present. That evening we introduced them to each other; Royston sitting on Margaret's lap and Olly sitting close beside on Joyce's lap. We arranged it this way purposely because during the course of the long stay with us, Olly has become extremely fond of our company, seeking physical contact with myself or Joyce whenever possible, and we were anxious that he should not become jealous of the new arrival. It was a very tense moment because we never like to expose any of the birds to unnecessary danger, but in the event they paid little attention to each other; Olly was more interested in flying on to Joyce's shoulder to preen her hair and Royston by now was too tired to care about anything.

The first few days passed fairly uneventfully. Royston ate all that was put before him, including fish, rabbit, pigeon meat and liver, and was growing rapidly. On 24 May, five days after his arrival, we weighed him on a set of baby scales borrowed from a friend. Unfortunately we had no initial weight to compare with, but he was now a handsome two pounds five ounce baby and capable of eating almost half his body weight each day. Our friend the butcher was very helpful but I needed a supply of fish and was extremely fortunate to find a manager of a fish shop in the local town who was prepared to save all the off-cuts and offal for me to collect each day. It was a messy business cutting out the large bones and fins and soon my car, the house in general and particularly Royston smelt like a trawler's hold; but it was the only practical answer to a very real problem.

To make life more interesting for him we would sometimes drop pieces of fish into a dish of water so that he could 'catch' them. He took food offered in this way but strangely he did not seem too keen on the water, and at that age he appeared to get all of the liquid he required from his food. I never ceased to be astonished at the vast quantity of fluid excreted when considering the relatively small amount taken in. It was certainly convincing proof that many so-called solids contain an amazing amount of fluid.

During this period it became obvious that it would not be practical for him to share the house with us for much longer and I spent a good deal of time preparing the garden shed for him. To allow ventilation I cut a section out of the door which I covered with wire and I also cemented over the earth floor so that I could wash the whole area clean more easily. The walls were of thick stone, which ensured that it was never too hot or really cold, and, with the addition of a layer of sawdust to absorb the droppings and a few large branches sawn from the apple tree for him to perch on, I felt that he would be happy. It was only about ten yards from the kitchen door and Joyce could look in on him frequently during the day. We had not previously allowed any of our birds away from continual contact with us but, as I have said before, this one was very different.

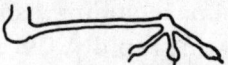

When I had completed the preparation to my own satisfaction I was keen to obtain an opinion from Royston and amid much cackling and struggling I carried him triumphantly down to the shed. I stood him in the doorway and he picked his way disapprovingly across the sawdust to the far corner, where he sat on his haunches looking disconsolate and dejected. He often sat in this manner, resting on his 'elbows' with toes spread in a pyramid like two giant spiders and tarsi about thirty degrees to the horizontal (see sketch). I waited for several minutes for him to get up to inspect his new home more closely, but he flatly refused to move and could not be induced to come for food which Joyce brought for him. He began to shiver nervously and therefore we decided to bring him back home in the hope that after a few more short visits he would accept the shed. It was quite clearly a bewildering experience for a young bird which should still have been in his tree-top nest, and he relaxed as soon as his immediate surroundings became familiar again, readily accepting the food he had so summarily refused moments before. He had come to rely on us entirely and showed great trust in us and we felt obliged to ensure that nothing would happen to destroy this close association – for the time being anyway.

Each day for the following three days, I took him into the shed and stayed in with him for half an hour or so in order to accustom him gradually to his new home and each time he became more interested in the objects around him. One by one he inspected the branches I had placed there until finally I left him on his own for a while and watched him through the key hole to ensure that he was happy. As soon as he accepted the shed as home, life was much easier all round. He had ample space to test his wings and exercise himself generally and we could return the house into something approaching normality.

He was growing at a phenomenal rate: on 24 May he had weighed two pounds and five ounces; by 12 June, having consumed nineteen pounds and four ounces of food in the twenty-day period, he weighed in at three pounds and thirteen ounces. I had no idea what the conversion ratio of food intake to body weight increase should be, but I thought it appeared fairly good and I was happy that Royston was looking in such good fettle.

During this period he had maintained a varied diet; this had included a six-inch roach, weighing about two ounces, which he took from my hand, lined up in his bill 'head-first' and swallowed whole. It was the first time in his life that he had encountered a complete fish and therefore I was impressed by the professional manner in which he had dealt with it. Another part of his feeding behaviour which intrigued me was the way in which he took food from the dish. Having prepared a quantity of fish, I used to feed him about four ounces at a time in an enamel dish which I placed just inside the door. He would rush across the shed, cackling wildly and come to a halt with madly flapping wings. He would then eye the food carefully, select a piece to eat and with a quick thrust, pull it from the dish and toss it on to the floor. Sometimes he would pick it straight up again and swallow it, other times he would watch intently for several seconds, as if waiting for it to move, before finally consuming it. This method of feeding necessitated clearing an area by the door or the food became covered in sawdust and was thus rendered inedible. I often wondered why he chose to throw his food out in this manner and I could only conclude that there would be distinct advantages in doing this when catching food at the water's edge because a fish, once thrown on to the bank, would stand far less chance of escape when lining it up to swallow than if the manoeuvre was completed over water. The lightning-quick jerk of the head when doing this would, I assume, be instrumental in killing the fish or animal anyway, and although he had not been taught any 'tricks of the trade' he appeared to know what to do.

All birds which are habitually abandoned by their parents at the nest (which include such species as swifts and guillemots) must be equipped with sufficient natural skill to feed themselves and this little fellow appeared to have all the answers.

Having settled him in the shed, my thoughts turned to making an outside run with a small pond so that he could prepare gradually for the final release. I considered several methods of doing this before deciding on the eventual design. So that he had the option of spending his time in the shed, which he now regarded as home, or taking the air in his run, I built it as an extension to the shed by erecting some poles and then fastening fruit cage netting to enclose an area six feet wide by twelve feet long. The shed door, when open, formed the closed door of the pen and in this way we could shut up the shed with Royston safely inside for the night and allow him free access to either during the day (see sketch).

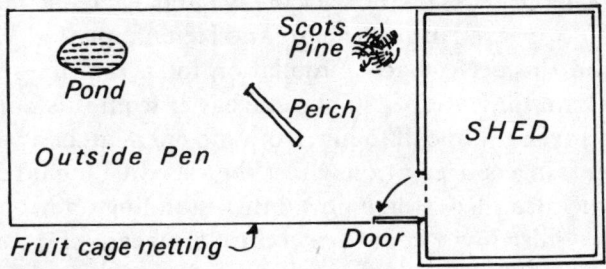

The actual construction of the pen was completed on the evening of 7 June and although it was too late when we had finished it to allow him out for very long, I was extremely keen to let him make an inspection. Joyce and I thought it was ideal; we had sunk an old galvanized bath into the ground and after filling it about half-full of gravel we had topped up with water to form a reasonable pond. There was sufficient space to introduce a branch from an elder bush for him to perch on and it still left room for him to wander about or rest beneath the small Scots pine that was growing within the enclosure.

He had been listening to all the activity and had cackled continuously; obviously anxious to find out what was happening. When, eventually, I opened the door he stepped cautiously out and, with considerable pomp, he strode sedately around the periphery. He then inspected the elder branch from end to end and finally moved across to the pond and dipped his beak in. I am sure he was pleased and I felt very excited as I saw him there, slightly more than half-grown, with water glistening on his beak and the late evening sun picking out the highlights of his plumage. He stretched his head and adopted the 'bottle of pop' stance. That was Joyce's description and in truth it filled the bill because when he adopted this pose his body resembled a perfectly symmetrical bottle, well-rounded at the bottom and supported by two rather stumpy legs.

I fetched some fish from the house to see if he would take it in his outside pen, and as I approached he became very excited and before I could place the dish on the ground I had collected a couple of fierce pecks on the back of my hand, each one drawing blood. He appeared in great shape and I felt happy that I had at last found the perfect accommodation for a rapidly growing heron. Communication also became easier from this point on, because Joyce could call to him from the open kitchen window and maintain a conversation whilst she was washing up or preparing the meal. Royston enjoyed this, standing on his branch cackling whilst Joyce kept up a continual stream of questions: 'What are you doing today then?' and similarly ridiculous questions, rather in the manner that mothers talk to their babies.

In this way relationships were closely maintained, but entry into his pen became an increasingly painful business. We were enjoying a magnificent spell of weather and I had abandoned formal clothing for more comfortable shorts and sandals. This gave Royston a very large target area for his constant jabs and soon my legs, hands and arms were peppered with tiny scars from the constant encounters with his bill. I do not think he really intended to do any harm because he did not appear vicious but his beak was such an efficient weapon that he could do considerable damage without even trying. I could tolerate the minor wounds inflicted, but I was conscious of the danger that a much more serious injury would result if he happened to strike at my eye; for this reason I took no chances with him and would not allow the children to get too close to the pen in case he managed to peck them through the netting.

As he grew he spent more and more time flapping his wings whilst standing on his branch, resting between times on his haunches under the shade of the pine tree or sunbathing with wings drooping beside him, eyes half-closed, with an air of ecstasy. Meanwhile, however, his beak became more powerful and my body more scarred.

One day, as I approached his pen with the usual dish of food, a mixture of liver and fish, he rushed towards the side of the netting with wings arched and head slightly bowed forward, cackling frenziedly. I did not go straight to the door but paused beside the pen face to face with him and with lighthearted mocking I leaned forward and cackled back. To emulate his posturing further, I thrust forward my hand and arm to simulate his beak and neck. Still cackling, he bowed his head lower until his beak almost rested on the ground whilst still maintaining the 'wings arched' pose. I followed suit and 'bowed' my outstretched arm – still cackling in return. As my hand neared the ground, his head was raised and so we alternated as if on either side of a seesaw. We continued in this manner for some minutes until finally he thrust his beak forward and we made contact through the netting. His beak gripped my fingers very gently and I realized that for the first time ever, we had secured a form of contact which allowed me to approach him without the usual painful consequences. When I entered the pen he stood quietly and took food from my hand with a gentleness I have rarely experienced. After he had fed he went to the pond to wash his beak and then retired to the shade to rest.

I sat beside him, trying to analyse what had happened. I was unable to reach any firm conclusions but I was convinced that somehow I had reached a level of communication with this bird never before experienced with any other. I was naturally keen to experiment again to test the difference between the direct approach and a meeting involving the 'greeting ceremony'. I also wanted an independent witness to the events, because I felt that a third party might spot something of significance that might elude me. Although the whole incident and subsequent behaviour when I entered the pen could well have been coincidental and not terribly significant, I was convinced that the interaction during the 'greeting ceremony' had resulted in my entering the pen without being attacked.

There was no point in returning immediately; I wanted him to settle down and wait for the next feed-time in the normal manner when, I hoped, the experiment would be valid. Displaying my usual impatience, I decided to go straight into the pen when the required time had elapsed, expecting him to peck me and then I could withdraw and try the 'greeting ceremony', thus combining two separate approaches almost simultaneously. When I did go in, with Joyce watching from the kitchen window, there was little doubt about his response and I bore a trickle of blood from my elbow as evidence. I withdrew quickly and retraced my steps across the lawn. I then immediately walked back to confront him through the netting, this time cackling in response to his calls and he went into the wings arched, head bowed, posture. I repeated the complete greeting ceremony and I had the feeling that the bowing of heads displayed a mutual submission, one to the other (of course what he was experiencing I had no idea). Again the ceremony ended when he thrust his beak forward to touch my hand and again he showed no aggression whatever when I entered the pen. This time there was no coincidence; it really worked. Although I was still unsure what we were actually saying to each other during this extremely comical greeting, the end result was very rewarding. I had never before experienced actual communication with a bird using their media, and the general thrill and satisfaction was indescribable.

I related the incidents to several of my close friends who remained singularly sceptical but one by one they all witnessed the ceremony under experimental conditions and had to accept that, for whatever reason, Royston's reaction was consistent. The only thing which disappointed me was that none of my friends would try the experiment themselves, explaining that it was sufficient for one of their friends to cackle and posture like a heron without making a general habit of it!

Throughout the period of his captivity, my friend who lived close to the heronry monitored the progress of the remaining young in the nest. In this way we could judge Royston's growth rate against the young raised under natural conditions and, perhaps more importantly, we could gain a fairly accurate idea of when he should be released. Royston, of course, had much more freedom than his brothers and sisters – not for them the little pond in the lawn to practise fishing, or the ample space to exercise in. They had a spacious nest but they were constantly squabbling for enough room to flap their wings and as yet it was suicidal to venture on to the branches.

We kept Royston as active as possible, and although it played an insignificant part in his diet we used to go to the river to catch minnows for him. What we had found to be sufficient to raise the kingfisher on only sufficed as an *hors d'oeuvre* for him though, and on one occasion we took cine-film of him eating fourteen minnows in not many more seconds. I still marvel at the incredible efficiency with which he used to catch his prey. Between feeds he continued to exercise his wings, flapping wildly whilst standing on his branch until he actually lifted from the ground. To give him further scope for trials I fixed a horizontal perch on to a post in the ground at one end of the run and from this he could make short flights. His wings were so massive that he could parachute from the perch to land as softly as thistledown a few feet away. I felt very confident at this stage that there was little else I could do for him and I sensed that he would soon be ready to go.

On 20 June, my friend telephoned to say that the young herons had left the nest – the moment of truth. Yesterday, I had been filled with confidence, viewing Royston as a father might view his son with pride before watching him embark upon the fortunes of life. Today suddenly it was all different. I was acutely aware that my feelings towards him were very much deeper than those of his true parents. Again I was tormented by all the uncertainties so inevitably associated with the final release and I knew I would not sleep soundly that night. In the event, nothing was more certain, for the weather changed and I lay thinking about the unfortunate young from the nest which were spending their first night alone in the appalling thunderstorms. Throughout the next week the storms continued. The rain lashed down on baked earth until, completely saturated, pools began to form on some of the low-lying land. Royston appeared completely unperturbed through all the storms, however, and often stood in the pouring rain for hours, shunning the shelter of the garden shed or the little tree in the corner. Even the thunder and lightning which sent the dogs diving for cover and barking in fear, was completely ignored and I began to question whether my decision to delay his release was wise. I argued that the wet wings would inhibit flight and lessen his chances of survival, but after several hours in the rain he could shake himself and appear dry and spruce again, so my argument lost its validity. In the end I decided that I would release him on Sunday morning, 1 July, whatever the weather. I had chosen Sunday because so many of my friends had become acquainted with Royston and wished to 'see him off', and that was the only day when everyone could be accommodated.

I had chosen the area to release him several weeks before. It had to be some way from my house because there was no water of any significance nearby and on the river Cherwell, below the village of North Aston, the confluence of the old mill race and the river formed an ideal fishing area for herons. The owners of the mill were pleased to learn that they might become guardians of Royston and I felt more confident when I knew that someone would be prepared to keep a watchful eye if he decided to remain there for a day or two. The adjoining field was flooded to a depth of about nine inches by the preceding week's rain and stacks of baled hay stood incongruously in the water.

We were to meet below the mill at nine am, giving me time to feed him a couple of times before setting off. I had also arranged for a friend of mine, John Woollett, who is a qualified bird ringer, to place a ring on his leg to allow future identification. The morning dawned fair and when I walked down the garden path to open the shed to greet him for the last time I felt that, despite my uncertainty, the moment was right. Large drops of

The author in his garden, with Royston's shed
and run in the background

Misty the mistle thrush, ready for his daily foot-bath in the sink

water still clung to the tips of the rose leaves which hung over the shed roof forming a jewelled archway over the door. Royston, far less emotional than myself, could only think of food and cackled loudly for his breakfast which he ate with relish. There only remained one problem now – getting Royston into the large cardboard box in which to transport him to the river. I knew that when I picked him up to place him in the box I would be very vulnerable to any pecks he might choose to aim at me. As I did not wish to alarm him any more than necessary, I decided not to try to place a hood over his head (the only certain way of avoiding damage) but relied on his friendly response to the greeting ceremony. Joyce stood ready to close the lid, and he let forth an ear-splitting squawk when I picked him up. Once in the box, however, he settled quickly and although he regurgitated some of his breakfast during the journey, he appeared none the worse on arrival at the mill.

I was even more apprehensive than usual when I saw the host of people who had collected to witness the release. I mentally counted a dozen heads, excluding myself, and rapidly tried to think of some way of explaining, without offending anyone present, that too many people might well disturb Royston. Fortunately they were all equally anxious not to interfere and therefore I set off from the car carrying the cardboard box, followed by one of my friends, Trevor, who was recording the event on cine-film. He was, in turn, leading the rest of the party in crocodile. We had only to walk about sixty yards from the road to the flooded field, and when everyone had discreetly hidden behind the parapet of a little bridge which connected the fields over a small stream I opened the box. Royston stood gazing around him, looking bewildered at the sunlit water, so different from his back garden pen. Not wishing to allow indecision at this stage I lifted him out, stood him in the shallow water and retreated a few yards to watch his reaction. He took a few cautious steps, then flapped his wings and I thought he would fly; but instead he decided to preen his feathers which had become slightly dishevelled from the journey and my handling him. As the minutes ticked away I became more anxious until eventually I felt quite guilty about the whole business. After about half an hour I decided to leave him alone for a while because he did not appear in any immediate danger and I thought he might settle more quickly if I was absent.

After six rather agonizing hours, Joyce and I returned and we quickly spotted him on the other side of the field. He appeared quite undisturbed and although he looked across at me when I called he made no attempt to come to me and even failed to respond when I cackled. I concluded that he was not too hungry or he would have come to me to seek food. Although he could easily have walked across the shallow floods I felt that he must have tried out his wings in the time he had spent there, so with a great deal of reluctance we tramped slowly back to the car to spend the night parted from his company.

He dominated all of our conversation that evening and I am sure that I would have gone back to see if he was all right had it not been a particularly dark night. I consoled myself with the fact that Mick Clist (the minnow-catching friend) would be calling to see him in the morning and by lunch-time I would have another report. Every telephone call at work the next day caused my heart to miss a beat until eventually I received the message that Royston had been sitting on top of a stack of bales in the field, at ten am sunning himself and preening. Mick had not delayed very long to watch him but at least he was alive and well, and despite the fact he was still in the same field he must have flown to secure his perch on top of the bales.

The reports continued to come in during the next few days as many of my friends re-routed their journeys to take in North Aston; Royston could be seen, usually on his favourite stack of bales or in the corner of the field near the river. As days turned into weeks the sightings became less frequent and it became harder to pick out the ring on his leg as he became more wary of visitors. On a visit to the area on 27 July, almost a month after his release, I saw him by the canal some 200 yards from the place of release, and although he allowed me to approach within about twenty yards of him, he then took to the wing and flew strongly back to his favourite field.

That should have been the end of the story because I really did not expect to see him again with certainty; but on a visit to the mill on 8 January, over six months after his release, I could see a couple of herons standing about a hundred yards apart beside the winter floodwater and I wondered if, just possibly, one of them could be Royston. I walked along the river bank towards them and immediately one of them flew off strongly downstream. I could see with my binoculars that it was a fully adult bird so that ruled out Royston, but the other bird, no more than seventy or eighty yards away, was clearly a bird of the year. He was watching me intently and I realized that he was about to fly any moment, so I trained my binoculars on him in the hope that I might catch a glimpse of a ring. The left leg was partially obscured as he took off, however, and I thought I had lost my chance. Instinctively I called his name and he swept in a wide circle back over the river and flew straight over my head. I still could not see a ring so, as he came over, I 'cackled' loudly and although he did not answer my call he cocked his head and looked down at me. I felt almost sure that it was Royston but the frustration of uncertainty was intense and I was terribly anxious to establish whether or not it was actually him. Again he flew in a wide circle but this time he came over low and landed near the little bridge where, just over six months before, we had parted company. As he lowered his landing gear I caught the glint of metal on his leg and in my excitement I moved towards him. Quite properly, the close bond between us had weakened and he immediately flew off again down river. I let him go without any further attempts to call him but this time I watched him with the true pride of a father watching his son embark upon a new life.

8

Green and gold

Life was exceptionally quiet without Royston. It was true that we still had Olly II whom I have mentioned briefly before, but his case was so similar to that of Olly I which has been described in a previous chapter that I will not repeat the details. It is sufficient to say that despite many occasions when we thought we had lost his company for good, especially when later in the year he spent his nights courting a rather smart female tawny from the nearby orchard, he still sits beside me as I write this book, glancing critically as each word is formed before finally trying to rip the corner of the page in a most disconcerting way. I still have high hopes that one day he will choose to leave us for good but meanwhile I have to be satisfied with the knowledge that he has never been confined in any way and enjoys the world outside, but prefers to roost indoors and to a great extent enjoy the easy living which we still provide.

We had, however, accepted as inevitable that a fairly constant stream of birds would arrive, and we only had to wait a couple of weeks for Pinky and Perky. The names given to the various birds are chosen in a variety of ways: they remind us of a human character we know in the village, or they have a call like 'sweet' the redpoll or, like Royston, they take their name from the rescuer; but with the case of the two little greenfinches, one was distinctly 'perky' and the other poor weakling looked positively 'pinky'.

I had been watching the progress of the builders on a new housing site in the village for some while with mild disapproval until eventually they had to remove a large hedge beside the road to make way for the road entrance. It was sad to see one of the important features of the village so ruthlessly destroyed. The birds which nested there each year had a trying time because a vast percentage of the children going to school found time to peer into the dense foliage in search of nests and, when they had located one, the tell-tale track soon invited other eager eyes to pry into the same spot; but inevitably a few succeeded each year and it gave the teachers at school a good opportunity to remind the children that they should not interfere with birds' nests and in this way a certain amount of good was achieved.

The heavy rains which fell in the week leading up to Royston's release were repeated later in the month and on the fifteenth, in the middle of a torrential downpour, one of the village lads arrived clutching two very muddy and bedraggled birds, explaining that he had retrieved them from the building site after the section of hedge containing the nest had been ripped out by the machine. They bore no signs of obvious injury but, being wet and cold, they were in grave danger of becoming chilled and dying as a result.

They offered very little resistance as I partially dried their feathers with a soft tissue and they gladly snuggled close to each other when I placed them in a small wicker basket which I had lined with an old woollen jumper. I judged that they were within two or three days of leaving the nest naturally, and was therefore hopeful that recovery would be quite speedy if they could sustain the shock of being thrown from the nest and the subsequent soaking.

As soon as they were warm and dry Joyce and I tried to feed them. Unlike many seed-eating birds which feed their young on insects and larvae, greenfinches regurgitate partially-digested food, and so we crushed some mixed breakfast cereal, moistened it with a little milk and force-fed a small amount to each. We popped them back into the basket for a rest while I prepared some finely-chopped egg moistened with glucose water and we thought that the combination of 'seed', milk, egg and glucose would revitalize them fairly quickly. It was very difficult to force sufficient food into them at any one time to consider it a reasonable feed, and therefore we had to keep up a more or less continual struggle, first inducing a small amount into one before going back to the other.

Very tiny birds gape for food instinctively at any sign of movement near the nest and adults will usually help themselves if given undisturbed surroundings, but at this half-and-half stage, the problems of feeding are generally most acute. It is a terribly frustrating business trying to force food into a bird whose only reaction is to resist all attempts and one can never judge whether sufficient or too much is being administered. There was no alternative, however, but to battle on until we had won their confidence in the hope that they would soon feed themselves, or at least respond to force-feeding.

By nightfall we could only hope that we had induced sufficient food inside them to last for a few hours. At least they had each other to help keep warm and I placed a small hot water bottle in the bottom of the basket. Inevitably I would have to get up during the night to offer food and change the hot water bottle but I hoped that they would be strong enough to go through until early morning without much attention.

At three in the morning, four beady eyes looked up into the sudden light and my heart gave a little flutter of excitement at finding them alive and well. I dipped the end of the eye-dropper into some already prepared cereal and milk and touched the beak of Perky with it, hoping for some response but, although the action stimulated a few cheeps of annoyance, he made no attempt to take the food. Joyce, who wakens in the night with great difficulty, staggered from bed to help me feed them and after twenty minutes or so we were questioning the value of wakening them from their warm bed.

Throughout the next day the tedious business of force-feeding continued and although Perky gained in strength and stature very quickly, Pinky seemed to be losing ground and we were very anxious about his condition. Inevitably the stronger one takes more food, which in turn speeds the road to recovery, and sadly the reverse holds true for the weaker patient. If Pinky could be induced to take food for himself and secure an interest in life, I felt that there was still hope for him but he moped in the corner of the basket and completely lacked the will to live. In desperation I went into the garden, collected a quantity of greenflies from the rose bushes and offered these as a pulp on the end of the eye-dropper. They made no attempt to help themselves but when Joyce opened their beaks so that I could place a little of the pulp in their mouths they swallowed readily. Following this partial success, I was tempted to try them with a couple of tiny mealworms and again these were accepted readily. After the feed I gave them a drink from the eye-dropper and was delighted when they began to chatter excitedly with the typical greenfinch twitter. Pinky proceeded to preen his wing feathers, and as a final encore to pronounce their joy they fluttered on to the edge of the basket, stretching and flapping in obvious contentment. Although there was still a long road to complete recovery, I felt that we had made a breakthrough and by late evening I was even more pleased to watch them scrambling over each other to peck at the eye-dropper which had been dipped in crushed breakfast cereal moistened with glucose water. Greenfinches are, by nature, greedy feeders and Pinky and Perky were beginning to show signs that they would be no exceptions. If one of them lost the tussle to get to the eye-dropper, it merely resorted to pecking off particles of food which had become attached to the other one's beak. When they had taken their fill in this manner, they would go for short excursions around the table and finally they would accept being placed in the basket where they settled for a short sleep. By bedtime I was beginning to feel quite confident and we planned the next stage.

They had effectively 'left the nest' and we felt that too much confinement at this stage might well inhibit their development; we therefore decided to allow them a certain amount of freedom in the room and also to fit perches in the box and supply food in the hope that they would begin to feed themselves. When we had completed the arrangements they were sleeping soundly with their heads tucked in and they remained that way until morning, not even waking when I checked them during the night.

By now they had accepted us completely and whilst we prepared a fresh dish of food they would fly on to our arms, chattering excitedly, unable to wait until it was ready for them. They appeared to enjoy being fed, although they had food in the box with them and we had seen them help themselves on several occasions. It was difficult to understand why they found so much excitement in being hand-fed but I was pleased to continue for a while because it gave the opportunity to be sure that each one had sufficient, and it also helped to establish the close relationship between us that I consider an important feature in the recovery.

The contrast between tending for two tiny greenfinches and looking after the needs of a huge heron is obvious, and the trend from large to small continued when two very young house martins arrived in the midst of the tea-time feed – just at the moment when we thought we had overcome the major difficulties and could settle down to a reasonable routine. It would be unfair to say that we are thrown into complete confusion at a time like this, but a casual observer might be forgiven for thinking so. Suddenly there is so much to do, so many things to collect together and so much to discuss. Some birds arrive in a reasonable condition and there is no immediate urgency to make snap decisions. The two little house martins were in very poor shape, however, being both cold and weak and very obviously in need of immediate care. The greenfinches were quickly ushered back into their box where, fortunately, they were quite at home and capable of fending for themselves for a while, and Joyce nestled the little martins in her cupped hands to warm them up whilst I made the little wicker basket ready to house the new occupants.

Breakfast-time the next day was as chaotic as I had feared it might be. In theory, I was to feed the greenfinches whilst Joyce tended to the needs of the house martins. In this way we could establish whether it was really practical for one person alone to feed them, before I left the house for work. Having prepared the food for both, I lifted the polythene hood from the greenfinches' box and they immediately scrambled on to the edge, calling loudly for food. It was not difficult to feed them, the only difficulty was maintaining a sufficient supply on the eye-dropper to satisfy their needs and keep them occupied. All was well until Joyce took one of the martins from the warm depths of their box to administer tiny pieces of liver. The greenfinches could not contain themselves – who were these intruders being given food by their own mother? As foster-father I was in no position to subdue their curiosity and possible resentment, and they immediately flew on to her hand with much chattering and excitement. Suddenly she had a rather nervous-looking little house martin surrounded by fluttering, twittering, demanding greenfinches and I am afraid that I could only look on and laugh. Soon, with no food forthcoming, the greenfinches began to search, rather hopelessly, farther afield and fluttered on to Joyce's shoulder from where they could make short sallies on to her head. The whole scene rather typified life at the moment but, with time pressing, I had to retrieve the greenfinches and return them to their box to help themselves in order to concentrate our efforts on the poor little martins.

The next week passed reasonably smoothly with all of them making good progress. The greenfinches were gradually gaining independence but up until now the only water they had received was the occasional drink from the eye-dropper, and I thought it was time to give them a regular supply so that they could drink when they wished, or bathe if they were so inclined. We gave them a shallow dish filled with about half an inch of water and Pinky flew down from his perch to inspect the new acquisition. He stabbed nervously at this new clear liquid before realizing the purpose and then proceeded to take a good drink, throwing his head back after each dip in professional style.

Perky had remained aloft, viewing events with great interest, and as if intent on outdoing his brother (or sister), he flew down eventually and hopped boldly on to the edge of the dish. As the dominant member of the brood, his reaction was quite different from Pinky's, and he launched himself straight into the middle – soon water was flying in all directions. I often wish my own children would wash with the obvious relish which birds show. He had just about enough depth to immerse his head and soon he was scooping up large quantities of water which ran in runnels down his back. At the same time his wings were working like pistons, drawing water up his flanks and on to his wing coverts to explode from the wing tips like water hitting a stone on a waterfall. As the excitement rose to a fever pitch, he stamped his feet and flicked his tail until he was totally immersed in a very effective water spray. By now even Pinky, who had returned to his perch which was placed about eighteen inches above the bottom of the box, was receiving quite a shower but although he watched with great interest he did not join in the fun.

All the signs were, that the miserable little bundles of wet feathers which had arrived at my home ten days earlier would soon be taking their rightful place in the wild. Admittedly it would be no good their looking for a good Samaritan with an eye-dropper full of crushed seed and glucose water to feed from, but they were taking more and more food themselves and I could see no problem in introducing them to the food they would find outside, thus making their task of food recognition as natural as their taking to the water.

We were rather relieved that during this period no newcomers had arrived, save for a badly damaged sparrow which was painlessly put to death; and a young robin, whose parents were anxiously calling to maintain contact with the other three members of the brood which we found near to the nest when, on my insistence, we returned to the site. The young had obviously just ventured out and I had suspected that the one brought to me was only the weaker member of a recently-fledged brood. So I had made the children take me to the site and gave them a

friendly, but strict, lecture about their behaviour, explaining
that they should have been aware that the parents were on
hand, that they were causing alarm and distress and probably
putting the other young in jeopardy. I allowed the children to
watch with my binoculars from a safe distance to see the
parents attending their young and soon all was back to normal
– the children, hopefully, would not make this all-too-common
mistake again.

July was drawing to a close and we had high hopes that when
the youngsters were off our hands we would be relieved of the
responsibilities of rearing orphaned birds. Undoubtedly there
would be other birds to take their place but the breeding season
was nearly over for the year. There were certainly no thoughts
about failure at this stage, everything seemed set fair for release
in the next week or so. When I came downstairs on the morning
of 30 July I received the same excited chatter from Pinky and
Perky, the usual contented 'chur' from the house martins, a
short hoot from Olly and life suddenly appeared strangely orderly and free from tension. I even gave myself priority and
made coffee before looking to the needs of the various bird inhabitants.

I had not been at work an hour when the telephone rang and
I could tell immediately from my wife's voice that something
was terribly wrong. For no apparent reason whatever, Pinky
had died. She found him dead in the bottom of the box,
moments after watching him feeding happily on the new batch
of seed she had just put in. She was naturally very distressed
and we decided that we must place Perky in a new box straight
away, giving him fresh covering in the bottom, new perches,
water dish and food, just in case some form of contamination
had caused Pinky's death.

It was a tragic loss and one which we never did explain, and
for several days afterwards we were very anxious about the welfare of Perky. If Pinky had died a fortnight earlier it would have
been easily accounted for, but under the circumstances it was
inexplicable and, we could not help feeling, inexcusable,

although how one insures against such an event I am not at all certain. The loss rate of young birds in the wild is quite staggering and it is fairly safe to say that if Perky eventually reached adulthood, our achievement would equal that expected under more normal circumstances; but we take this as little consolation and each loss is registered as a black mark in the notebook I keep.

In the event there were no further disasters, and our attention turned to preparation for release. For Perky it was just a question of collecting grasses, plantain seed-heads, docks, clover seed, etcetera, in an attempt to ensure that he could relate the natural sources of food to what he had previously eaten.

The release was successfully completed from the garden on 8 August, and only three days later Joyce experienced the indescribable pleasure of seeing Perky contentedly preening on the buddleia bush. Strangely he was a little nervous of her presence and after a few moments flew confidently away down the field and into a nearby orchard. We did not see him again, but he had firmly taken his life into his own hands, displaying the confidence he had always shown and we were extremely pleased to settle for the knowledge that he no longer needed us.

I was grateful for the experience we had gained whilst raising the young greenfinches when, recently, we had to face the fearful prospect of dealing with five extremely young goldfinches. The nest had been beautifully constructed in a large lilac bush in a garden only a short distance from my house. The previous owners of the house had given little thought to the placing of the shrub and it had quickly outgrown the space available, so the present occupant had taken very positive action to remedy the situation by removing the bush. Sadly, he had been unaware of the goldfinches' nest and he had not even noticed it as he cut branches down with his secateurs. It was not until one of the final twigs fell away from the bare framework that the nest was discovered: now lying on the lawn, with terrified young still clinging to the sides. I have learned to accept most situations but the sight of a man, concern carved in the expression on his face, clutching a short piece of lilac branch containing a nest of five young goldfinches, standing at my door, left me speechless. He was so anxious to explain the situation and justify the reason for his presence, that he spluttered the story out whilst still standing on the doorstep.

We discussed the possibility of rebuilding the bush, using wire to attach the branches to the remaining trunk, but his efficiency with a pair of secateurs had put this beyond hope, and with a great deal of apprehension I took them in, hoping that they would respond at least as well as the greenfinches.

To list the complete details of their stay with us would only duplicate much of the story of the greenfinches, and it is sufficient to say that the three larger birds, still completely devoid of feathers on their arrival, responded well to a mixture of porridge made from 20 mls of crushed Alpen (a mixed breakfast cereal), 2 mls glucose, one spot of Abidec (multi-vitamin drops) and 25 mls of water. We found that this could be offered from the end of a partially-sharpened matchstick and we had only to touch the side of the nest which, for convenience, we had stood in a copper rose-bowl, to bring wobbly heads and necks craning up for the expected meal. The food we gave them was both easily prepared and satisfied their needs, producing an acceptable proportion of bright, healthy young goldfinches, but it should not be considered adequate because we lost one of the greenfinches and two of the goldfinches. I am still baffled by the fact that the survivors appear to lack nothing and can eventually cope with life beyond the home, but until the percentage of failures can be reduced I cannot feel entirely satisfied.

9

Misty and the neurotic blackbird

The following autumn and winter proved to be a quiet time with regard to birds. A couple of adult kestrels had been brought to us with symptoms of poisoning, but happily they had recovered very quickly, responding well to good food, rest and a course of antibiotics which we give to all birds in poor condition as preventive medicine rather than for any specific cure.

With the arrival of spring, however, the situation changed completely and dramatically. Early in April, Misty, a young mistle thrush, and Blackie, an almost fully-grown blackbird, arrived practically simultaneously. Misty had been found crouched beside a busy 'A' road near my village and, although I tried to locate the nest and put him (or her) back in the vicinity of his parents, I could find neither the nest nor adult birds and therefore I was compelled to foster him. He still had tufts of downy feathers above his eyes and his stumpy little tail was edged white – in fact he was a very white-looking bird, altogether, even for a mistle thrush. He was extremely alert and, as soon as food was offered, lost no time in devouring a hasty meal.

Nothing could have been more different than Blackie, who arrived the next day. He (or she) was the surviving member of a brood of four and he had watched helplessly as the three other members had been killed by a marauding cat. Miraculously, having been seized himself, he had lived whilst the cat was being chased around the garden, but he was in very poor shape when he eventually arrived at my house. Several tail feathers were missing and the feathers on his breast were wet and dishevelled. We made no attempt to feed him but placed him quietly in a cardboard box for him to recover from his shock and I do not think that we gave very much for his chances. After about an hour we decided that he should be fed, but he tucked his head nervously into the corner of the box and struggled frantically when I picked him up. Having got him out, we decided that we might as well give him some food and, despite all his efforts at resistance, we forced him to swallow a good-sized earthworm which had been crushed and broken into about five pieces; he was then placed back in his box to rest, and I hoped the realization would dawn that we wished him no harm.

We turned our attention again to Misty, who was by now calling loudly for food again, and although processing worms to feed to birds is best not described at meal-time, I consider it worthy of mention within this text. Just about everybody has, at some time, watched blackbirds hauling worms out of the lawn for consumption, either by themselves or for their nestlings, but very few people note the meticulous care with which they kill each one, break it into manageable pieces and then extract most, if not all, of the soil content in the worm's gut. Adult birds are not necessarily quite so fastidious when taking worms for their own consumption, but I think the removal of soil from the worm which is being prepared for young birds serves to reduce the amount of indigestible material given and also (probably coincidentally) reduces the chance of passing on disease which may be carried in the soil.

The most effective way to emulate the parent birds' treatment of a worm is to lay it between two sheets of newspaper and then, starting at the front end, systematically crush it with pressure applied by the thumb, thus removing the soil, which is ejected at the back end, and killing the worm. It can then be broken into several pieces, the size dependent upon the age of the bird, from about a quarter of an inch long for really small birds until eventually there is no need to break it up at all. It is a time-consuming process but we have found it to be justified when comparing the success rate of birds fed on this diet against birds which were fed with uncrushed worms in the early days. It is always difficult to generalize, but I think it is fair to say that success depends to a great extent upon attention to details, and this applies to the degree of hygiene surrounding the birds as well as to their diet. This is one of the reasons I favour keeping sick birds in cardboard boxes which can regularly be destroyed and replaced, so the chances of a build-up of infection can be limited.

Certainly Misty's box needed changing regularly – he had a really healthy appetite and, even when the newspaper covering on the bottom of the box was replaced several times a day, it was necessary to wash his feet most evenings to remove the trampled droppings. He appeared, however, to enjoy his foot bath and invariably took a drink from the running tap whilst I scrubbed away with a soft nail-brush. It was an incongruous sight but it did the trick, and after a while he would even fly from the box to the sink in anticipation.

Both Misty and Blackie were kept in the kitchen for warmth, April that year being a particularly cold month; although they were in separate boxes, they could obviously hear each other call and I thought that they would eventually become used to each other and co-habit the kitchen without any problems. We had been very gentle with Blackie at all times, never making any sudden noises near his box or startling him with extravagant movements when handling him, and very gradually he was beginning to settle down and take a bit more interest in life. Feeding him was still a strain because he hated being handled but, as he flatly refused to eat himself, he left us with little alternative. When returned to his box he would scurry back into the corner and sit there, ostrich-like, with his head buried for several minutes before venturing back on to his perch.

Misty's response at the end of a feed was totally different. He would sit on his perch and sing a contented little song as if to say how pleased he was. I considered I knew mistle thrushes in the wild quite well but I had never heard this song before as it was only discernable at very close range, and can only be described as the softest of soft warbling songs I have ever had the pleasure of listening to. Sometimes it was necessary to place one's ear within a foot or so to hear it, but to me it was as good as any nightingale – but then I was biased!

Like all infants, Misty spent much of his day asleep at this stage, waking frequently for feeds, then shortly falling back into a light slumber. During the periods in which he was neither asleep nor hungry, he would explore his box and I was intrigued by the way he would cock his head on one side and peer intently at the newsprint on the paper, then from time to time stab at imaginary worms which perhaps he thought he could see. I was greatly encouraged by this behaviour as it clearly illustrated that the rather distinctive manner in which thrushes seek food is instinctive rather than taught. He would still have to accompany Joyce into the garden on foraging trips later on to sharpen his reflexes, but at least he had the right approach.

The foraging trips are greatly enjoyed by all the birds which participate, and the eagerness with which they await the next worm being found is very obvious. In the early days we used to venture forth with a fork or trowel and dig frantically in the borders for worms, in the hope that it would encourage the birds to search similar areas for themselves, but we have since modified the practice to make it easier for ourselves and more instructive for the birds. We first bury a shallow tray containing a few worms in the garden so that our search is much more limited and also more positive and then we can probe with our fingers in a manner much more closely related to that expected of the young birds. At first they will stand and stamp their feet, craning their necks eagerly forward, waiting for the hidden treasure to emerge, but eventually they will join in the digging, and then real progress has been made.

The endless debate as to whether young birds should be allowed to become so tame that they can be safely taken into the garden at an age when they are capable of flight, and thus face the danger of not fearing man; or whether they should be kept in fear of physical contact, and then face the problems of hunting food with no tuition, cannot be readily resolved, but I remain firmly convinced that a foster-parent should attempt to play the role of the true parent as far as possible and this of course necessitates a close mental and physical association.

Misty, then, was establishing the pattern of behaviour which we had hoped for and which we look upon as normal. The problem of breaking down the barrier which existed between Blackie and the world in general was a much more difficult task. We felt he had slumped to the depths of hopelessness within himself and he wanted to crawl away to die. We could not explain to him that life held much to offer, his faith had been so badly shaken, nor could we analyse his problems in the way that a psychiatrist might operate with a human being – we could only patiently await the day when something would restore his confidence.

For about a fortnight he remained in this unhappy condition, feeding only when forced to, refusing to bath and generally shunning any attempt to touch him. For Misty, the day was one long round of pleasure and in the evening he would come out to take his bath before flying on to Joyce's shoulder to shake and preen. Blackie had always ignored the boisterous activity and noise associated with Misty's evening ritual, but we were suddenly thrilled when he hopped from the corner of his box on to the perch and called loudly as Misty flew busily from the kitchen sink to the table and back again. We hardly dared hope that he might want to come out and join in, but we carefully removed the polythene hood from his box in case he should venture out. He hopped first on to the side of the box, then flew up on to the table, peering nervously around, aware of the nerve-racking situation he had committed himself to. He crouched in obvious fear when Misty swooped over him *en route* to Joyce's shoulder, but he stood his ground and even plucked up the courage to examine the breadcrumbs on the table. It was a faltering, tense and almost unwilling start but it was a major breakthrough and we hoped that it would be the foundation upon which his complete recovery would be built.

The strain of his sudden exposure to the outside world, albeit the rather limited world of a small kitchen, was beginning to show and we therefore placed him back in the box, adding a saucerful of crushed worms in the hope that he would attempt to feed himself to cap his first splendid effort. As always, we had hoped for too much, but within two or three days he was enjoying an increasing amount of freedom and looking for his meal when he returned to his box.

His nervousness was very deep-seated: until his final release he would always scuttle to the corner of his box at any sudden loud noise and was never too happy about being handled, but his initial inhibitions gradually waned and he developed a gentle character different from, but as acceptable as, that of the bold, boisterous Misty.

I have explained before that birds vary tremendously as individuals and I still had faith that Blackie would gain the confidence necessary to take him out into the wild; what we could not hope to do was to take him into the garden like the other young thrushes we had kept. A similar technique can be applied to determine their ability to fend for themselves, however, and in Blackie's case 'plan B' had to be put into operation. A much larger box was prepared to take all the necessary fixtures and, because of the ultimate weight, it had to be put in a permanent position. We first lined the lower half of the box with polythene to waterproof it and then added about an inch or so of soil. Part of the soil was subsequently turfed over and into one corner of the remainder we sank a pyrex dish filled with water for drinking and bathing. Two perches were placed, one at either end, so that most of the floor remained free from droppings, and small worms were then tossed in on top of the moist soil for him to catch and eat. For the first couple of days we still hand-fed him several times during the day, but we would watch through a spy-hole in the side of the box and were well pleased with the way he took worms which were lying on the surface. Several, inevitably, found their way into the soil and under the turf and he soon became aware that movement in the soil suggested the presence of a worm. Gradually we reduced the amount hand-fed, and he became more and more proficient at catching the worms under ground whenever he felt hungry. Whether his decreasing reliance upon us helped him to establish greater confidence generally, I do not know, but he certainly appeared less nervous and after a week of this treatment it would have been difficult to persuade a casual onlooker that he had been any other than a perfectly normal blackbird.

He tended to ignore Misty's incessant churring, treating him rather contemptuously, and this again pleased me for it was no good merely being able to find food if he was going to allow other birds to chase him away. In open competition he was obviously never going to be a match for Misty, but from our observations in the wild, when mistle thrushes and blackbirds are feeding together, the blackbirds are automatically lower in the peck order so there was really no value in trying to establish equality at home. I have long assumed that much of the food taken by blackbirds is introduced into their diet by watching other more experienced birds, because when the young are hatched in April, May or June there are no fallen apples, raspberries, blackberries, etcetera, available. Therefore I could see little benefit in trying to vary his diet too much but, mainly as an experiment, I halved a large apple, which we had stored from the previous year, and gave a portion each to Blackie and Misty. Misty immediately pecked at his and dragged it around his box, mainly I think, because it was a new introduction and he was inquisitive. At first he ignored the pieces which dropped off but later, when he had tired of his game, he pecked at them and tried to swallow one piece. When he found it to be palatable he ate the rest, suggesting a rather trial and error approach to the problem. Blackie, on the other hand, ignored his apple for a long while, being very suspicious of anything new, but after a couple of hours he began to peck at the fleshy interior and immediately swallowed the pieces which broke off. I am certainly not going to try to draw any conclusions from their different behaviour with the apple, but it is yet another illustration of their different approach to life.

As both of them were fully capable of finding their own food and in splendid physical condition, it was time to plan for their total release. The moment of parting is always a heart-rending experience despite the fact that we have striven towards this ultimate goal throughout the stay, and we try to choose a location suitable for each individual where they can find food, water and natural cover in their chosen environment. The local woods seemed to fit the bill for Misty, for there he would find not only the necessities of life but company of his own kind, because each year we watch the post-breeding flocks collecting on the yew trees near the lake. Confidence radiated from him and, though he would undoubtedly feel alone and unsettled for a few days, he would be able to live on his fat reserves until he had found the right feeding spots.

To the bitter end we worried about the fate of Blackie, and in his case we thought that it would be better to liberate him in the garden so that, if necessary, we could keep an eye on him and put food out should he require assistance. Another factor which prompted this decision was the extremely dry weather which had continued throughout the winter, spring and early summer period. Worms would be difficult to come by in many localities, but I had continually watered the lawn in order to make my nightly catch of worms after dark and this meant relatively easy pickings for the local thrush population. Also we could scatter a few partly-rotten apples underneath the shrubs in the border to supplement the food supply, giving him the best possible chance of success. There was naturally no guarantee that he would stay in the garden but we had dictated his life long enough and the great test could not be put off any longer.

We released Blackie on the morning of 6 May, by placing his box beneath the lower branches of an old Lawson's cypress tree and removing the polythene cover, leaving it to Blackie to decide when to leave and where to go. As we had suspected, he did not go far for the first few days but gradually we saw less and less of him, and I can only assume that eventually he moved out, probably encouraged to do so by an old male who heralded his presence from the top of the birch tree; a couple of days later we found his mate's nest in the honeysuckle on the side of the shed. Blackie was no competitor in this type of situation and I am quite sure that he decided to slip discreetly away rather than stay and defend his home and food supply. Whether, in the final analysis, we had sufficiently prepared him for such harsh realities, I shall never know. Naturally I hope he found himself a niche, but I would be untruthful if I did not admit to some misgivings about his future.

On the same evening of 6 May we took Misty to the chosen woodland fringe and, armed with a camera to take a few last pictures, we opened the box carefully so that he could view his new surroundings. In a flash he had assessed the situation, and he flew straight into the top of a very tall elm tree.

We took our photograph, with a telephoto lense, and although I am the only one who knows the real significance of that tiny silhouette against the evening sky, it will always conjure up a very fitting climax to a very enjoyable episode.

10

Barney

As a lad, I found nothing unusual in listening, as I lay tucked in bed, to the loud shrieking of the barn owls which nested in the farm buildings near my home, and indeed, I expected to see one fairly frequently if I went badger-watching on the edge of Thenford wood. Not that I never see a barn owl now; I have to be content with a fleeting glimpse of one making over the hedge away from the startling car headlights, and even these occasions are becoming increasingly rare and unpredictable.

It is generally agreed that the decline in numbers began in about 1947, and undoubtedly the increased use of persistent toxic chemicals in farming, which were passed on to the larger birds via their prey, was a significant factor in their partial disappearance from the countryside.

Barn owls are beautiful creatures; but their wild shrieks and silent ghostly flight, the suddenness with which they can appear and then melt back into the darkness, give rise, I am sure, to many ghost stories, and many country children have secret fears about these birds. My wife's introduction to barn owls was both sudden and terrifying. We had only met a few months previously and one warm, pleasant autumn evening, I suggested that we should take a walk to Thenford. Dusk was falling as we approached the wood and it was with considerable trepidation that she entered the dense gloom and accompanied me along the path, over the brook, and on past the church under the canopy of large beech and aspen trees. The moorhens and coots were saying their final 'good-nights' down on the lake and the odd rustle among the leaves on the woodland floor suggested that the small rodents were emerging for an evening snack, safe from the flurry of the day. I had enjoyed sublime relief from the tensions of the day by walking through the wood in the late evenings on countless occasions, but Joyce found the experience far from relaxing, and when I suggested that we should sit for a short while on the low wall which surrounds the old churchyard, I could sense a very real reluctance to 'hang around in the eerie place'. I found her response difficult to appreciate and tried hard to explain the excitement of allowing oneself to become absorbed in the woodland atmosphere and fuse into the environment in a way which is difficult to achieve during daylight hours, when a human being is so much more obvious and the other creatures so much more aware of the human presence.

I thought I was beginning to succeed until a white shape drifted silently around the tall conifers on the far side of the churchyard, paused momentarily over one of the large gravestones to question the appearance of two strange figures on the wall, and then effortlessly drifted on, to be engulfed in the darkness.

I felt very excited that on our first walk to Thenford I had been able to show Joyce a barn owl but although her first 'real live ghost' had completely rendered her speechless, she soon regained co-ordination of her limbs and I followed her back down the path considerably faster than we had approached. During the mile-long walk back home I did little to convince her that she had been extremely fortunate, and it was many years before she savoured the joy of walking through the wood in darkness.

It was to be twenty years before she made more than a nodding acquaintance with a barn owl again, but then the circumstances were totally different, and Joyce was very much in control of the situation. Barney arrived at lunchtime on 10 January, 1975, and as he lay on his back in a cardboard box, he looked more dead than ghost-like. The two men with him had taken a great deal of trouble to find our house and bring him to us but he (or she) was in very bad shape and the long delay in finding warmth and rest had probably been a contributory factor to the way he looked. He had been picked up beside the road some twenty miles from my home (coincidentally, only a few hundred yards from the spot where Fishy had been found), and had then journeyed to London and back (a round trip of no less than a hundred and twenty miles), before finally sensing the warmth and security of Joyce's hands. He was barely conscious, and although there was no apparent injury and he was too plump and well groomed to be suffering from disease or poisoning, he felt very cold, and without help it was difficult to believe that he could survive much longer. He was totally unresponsive as Joyce settled him on her lap by the fire and cradled her hands over his back.

Although patience and warmth had worked so often in the past, little progress had been achieved by tea-time, when I first learned of our new arrival from Trevor. Joyce had been content to sit with Barney for the first three hours but, sensing that some degree of improvement should have been discernible by then, she decided to telephone Trevor for help. He was requested to call at the shop for instructions from me, before going on to Joyce, and in this way someone could be with her a full hour and a half before I arrived back from work. I felt that neither Trevor, nor myself, would be able to do anything beyond what was already being done, but at least Joyce would be able to discuss the problem and in this way, relieve some of the tension she was obviously feeling.

After Trevor left me I felt anxious to get home and the remainder of the afternoon appeared eternally long. I expected to find Barney still on Joyce's lap when eventually I did get home but although Trevor was still there, I could see no sign of the owl. I soon learned that he had recovered consciousness and had taken a small feed before being placed in a warm box. He was not able to stand and therefore Joyce had placed an old jumper to pad the sides of the box which secured him in a comfortable position, and the situation was much more encouraging than I had expected to find. We discussed the matter over a cup of coffee before giving him a further small feed, and when we placed him back in the box for the second time, he was able to stand for a short period on uncertain legs before settling back into the hollow formed by the jumper. We could only conclude that he had been suffering from concussion, caused probably by colliding with a vehicle while patrolling the roadside at dawn. The only other explanation which appeared possible was that he might have been caught in the very powerful slipstream of a fast-moving lorry and tossed to the ground – rather less likely than actually colliding, we thought, but I had seen this happen to a pigeon, which remained in a dazed condition for hours before recovering properly. The main thing, however, was that he was responding slowly to the treatment Joyce had offered and his condition was becoming less worrying as each hour passed.

I had never studied a barn owl in close-up, and the black-tipped white spots which embroidered his golden head and wings were as beautiful as drops of rain on a sunlit window. The facial disc was sharply edged with black-tipped feathers, and the ridge of feathers which separated two black eyes accentuated the gleaming hooked bill beneath. He was certainly a striking bird and I hoped very much that we would soon see him in full splendour, ready to tackle the outside world again.

It seemed pointless to force any further attention on him until he had rested for the night, and we transferred him to the warmth of the kitchen to spend his first night in enforced captivity. As always I was anxious to be up early the next morning and I was both thrilled and relieved to find him standing quite confidently in the corner of the box when I peered in. Our conviction of the day before, that he had been struck by a vehicle, was fairly certainly confirmed when I spotted a large pellet in the box which he had cast during the night – proof that he had fed normally before being found. When I reached in to pick up the pellet for examination, he spat and snorted at me, leaning back into the corner of the box with legs thrust forward and talons menacingly poised to strike. I had hoped to see him in full splendour soon, and he was fast becoming the bird one more readily thinks of when conjuring up thoughts of an owl.

I went back upstairs to tell Joyce the good news and suggested that she should come down, despite the early hour, to try to feed him again. Whilst I was waiting for her to join me in the kitchen I offered him some raw beef, but although he was ready to snap at anything which came within range, including my finger, he refused to swallow any, and it was soon obvious that we would have to force-feed again; this time, however, I felt that we would be facing problems which had not been apparent the evening before. I placed a piece of beef at his feet to see if this would encourage him to feed, but he chose the wrong piece of meat and buried his talons in my finger, locking on with a deadly grip which had surely seen the end of many a small rodent in the past. I did not wish to excite or distress him and therefore I remained in that rather painful position until Joyce appeared on the scene, muttering about my stupidity for allowing myself to be compromised so easily, and pottered off to find some gloves before making any attempt at a rescue. The relief was infinite when eventually she picked him up and I managed to extricate my finger from his grip but before proceeding with the proposed feed we held a quick consultation as to how this would be best achieved.

With his extraordinarily long legs, he could strike with his talons at any object near him, and therefore it was essential to anchor his feet, before tackling the prospect of pushing meat into a very powerful beak. We found that by sitting him on a towel on my lap, with his head facing my right shoulder, and Joyce gently covering his feet with one gloved hand, whilst supporting his back with the other, he was well positioned for me to feed him. The technique was to allow him to snap at a piece of meat and then, with the left hand, force the beak open, and push the meat down with the index finger of the right hand. This appeared to work very well, and although he did not relish the idea of being handled, we at least had the satisfaction of knowing that he was getting food, and judging by the remarkable progress he had made in the few hours with us, he would not have to be subjected to this treatment too often. We were further consoled by the knowledge that most adult birds will feed themselves, once they are capable, if they are left alone in quiet, undisturbed surroundings.

When Joyce returned him to the box after a hearty meal he fell into the corner on his back with his legs pushed stiffly forward, and it was not until I had become entangled with his talons yet again that we realized he was not still suffering from lack of balance, but had adopted this position as a natural defensive gesture. As soon as we placed a newspaper over the box and the threat of human presence was gone, he scrambled to his feet and jumped on to the log which I had placed in the box for him to roost on.

I felt that he would be perfectly at home in his box during the day – a place probably not dissimilar from his chosen roosting place in the wild – but it was becoming increasingly plain that he would not be content to remain in strict confinement during the coming night.

That evening we cleared the kitchen of all potential hazards and, after force-feeding a light meal, he was left with meat in his box in case he chose to stay put, but the covering was left off, and I placed a mixture of pulped beef and rabbit fur on the kitchen table, which I felt sure he would find if he ventured out. Knowing how keen tawny owls are to bathe regularly, I had also placed on the floor a large shallow tray containing about an inch and a half of water which, I thought, would be ample for drinking and just about adequate for a bath if he felt the need.

Our bedroom is situated immediately above the kitchen, and I was just about to doze off when I clearly heard the flap of wings against the box and I knew he was beginning the exploration of the room. I lay there for quite some time, listening for further tell-tale noises which might indicate his whereabouts, but eventually I fell asleep none the wiser, and it was not until Olly II appeared at the bedroom window from his nocturnal wanderings at about seven-fifteen, that I was really conscious again. I dressed hurriedly to the accompaniment of a few hoots and twitters from Olly, and when I opened the door to go downstairs he flew across on to my shoulder for a lift to the living-room. As Olly made for the television, his chosen roost, I made for the kitchen to see what had happened there.

The box was empty, but for the meat which I had left for him; the beef and rabbit fur was still on the table and the floor was dry around the water dish, but there was no sign of the bird. I looked around frantically and finally spotted him pressed against the wall, sitting on top of the small water-heater over the sink. How to retrieve him from up there? I put on the gloves which had been left in readiness and got a chair to stand on so that I would be at a more comfortable height and, as soon as I was in position, he slid silently over my shoulder and landed firmly on the table – this was not going to be so easy. Not wishing to panic him, I eased myself off the chair and as I approached, he flung himself into the typical defensive posture, leaning against the refrigerator which adjoins the small table. I stretched my left hand forward and felt his talons bite deep into the leather glove; by discarding the right glove, I managed to collect him up and place him in the box. In many respects the night had been spent successfully, but he had not eaten, and therefore Joyce had to be called in for assistance.

It was obvious that his recovery was almost complete and we could think immediately of his return to the wild, but on the other hand I felt that a few days' rest, with easy feeding and plenty of warmth, would improve his chances of success when returned to his former haunts. Although he had flown from the water-heater to the table, it was not to be compared with the sustained flight which would be necessary to secure his food. It was true that I had found a few droppings on the table, but the indications were that he had flown up on to the water-heater early on in the night and had remained there for many hours. Both Joyce and I concluded that we should, in some way, try to assess his flight potential before the release, and we thought that this could most easily be achieved by giving him the freedom of the lounge during the evening, when we could sit quietly with him and, hopefully, watch him fly relatively unhindered. I had told Ian (who had taken so many wonderful black and white photographs in the past) about our new acquisition and he was keen to record him on film, so long as the bird did not become distressed by the presence of a camera and a further stranger, and Trevor was equally anxious to test his response to cine-film. I warned them both that the chances of actually photographing such a wild creature were fairly remote, but they had spent many abortive hours at my house before, always giving absolute priority to the welfare of the birds, so I was not concerned by the fact that they would be calling to see Barney.

Trevor arrived first, in the event, and we agreed that he could at least film Barney being force-fed, because we had decided to do this prior to his liberation in the larger room. He had settled down very significantly, and took his food remarkably well, offering no resistance and swallowing each piece readily. He totally ignored the cine-camera and the extra lighting we had brought in, and when we were satisfied that he had had sufficient, he flew up on to the ledge of the window which is situated in the wall between the hall and lounge. After a long pause, he floated (and that is the only truly descriptive word I can find) out into the room, hovered effortlessly on barely moving, silent wings, before alighting gently on the top of my desk. I had been used to a large tawny owl gliding around the house, when often the movement of air as he passed was the only indication that he was in flight, but I had never witnessed a bird move with such effortless ease, and with such absolute silence. I was thrilled by what I had seen and I would have loved the opportunity to watch him through the night as I had watched Olly previously. My presence through the night would have seriously inhibited his movements though, and I felt that I would have to be content with a few brief hours in the evenings during the next couple of days or so.

Barney was adjusting to his new environment very well and it was not long before he made a return trip to the window-ledge, and from there to the chair-back on the far side of the room. It must have felt good to sense the buoyancy of flight again and we knew that it would be improper to keep him in captivity much longer. Saturday the eighteenth was agreed as a provisional date for release, thus giving him the remainder of the week to build up his strength and confidence, and Trevor and I agreed to meet at Weston-on-the-Green at eight pm on the chosen day, hoping that Barney would be able to re-establish himself in his familiar territory. I telephoned Ian to inform him of the plans, and he agreed to call the next evening, at feed-time, to take some photographs. We were still having to force-feed, Barney flatly refusing to help himself, but with a well established routine this was accomplished without any bother, and although he always snorted and hissed at Joyce as she lifted him from the box he displayed very little real aggression when I gave him the meat.

Like me, Ian was very intrigued by Barney and when he subsequently approached him in the window to take his photograph I could only watch in amazement at Barney's reaction. He first partially arched his wings and with his head swaying slowly, but deliberately, from side to side, he emitted the most fearful noises. I did, in fact, capture these on tape, and I still listen with disbelief that a bird could produce such a weird vocabulary. He began with the usual snorts and hisses, interposing a few sharp snaps of the bill, but then built up to a crescendo, rather like a whistling kettle approaching boiling point. After several minutes, he tucked his head right down between his legs, 'snoring' quietly, and then looked up again, hopeful, it would have seemed, that the problem had gone away during his 'absence'. It had not, so he went straight back into the head-swaying routine, this time with wings arched higher, and I was surprised that steam did not appear from his nostrils. I warned Ian that I was not certain how long this could continue before he actually struck at him but Ian, like myself, was conscious of the need not to over-excite him and so he withdrew a few paces.

Barney immediately relaxed and flew nonchalantly on to the desk, obviously happy that any threat had passed, and from there he flew on to the floor and made a careful examination of my briefcase which was tucked under the table by the window.

It had been an exciting few moments, savouring the full potential of a barn owl, so different from the cold, useless bundle of feathers which had been presented to Joyce a few days earlier. This was the bird we had hoped to see and we felt extremely grateful for the opportunity.

Barney's next few days were spent similarly, and in the most part, uneventfully, and the only further surprise was the way in which both Barney and Olly completely ignored each other. We naturally did not risk allowing the two birds together in the same room, but quite often during the evenings Olly would decide to hoot quite loudly, clearly audible in the kitchen, and Barney was not averse to the occasional snort, or even screech. But neither of them showed the slightest reaction to the other, quite unlike the immediate reaction Olly displays if he hears a little owl, when his body stiffens, and he strains his ears in the direction of the sound. I had always assumed that there would be a certain amount of competition for food and nesting sites between the two species, and had fully expected Olly to be quite annoyed by the presence of a barn owl on his territory, but if this was the case he certainly hid his feelings successfully, not even bothering to open an eye if he was pretending sleep.

Saturday dawned fair, and as we were enjoying the mildest winter in living memory I felt no compunction about releasing Barney in the evening. The weather forecast was for a slight frost, but he was in wonderful condition and with a clear, starlit night, I was sure that he would enjoy good hunting. We gave him a good feed when I returned from work in the evening, which would sustain him if necessary, so there was little to feel concern about. The only thought which bothered me was the fact that he was obviously used to hunting in the vicinity of a busy 'A' road and he had fallen victim to one of the many vehicles, but wherever we chose he would encounter various

Treasures unearthed – but Misty must learn to find
worms for himself before he is released

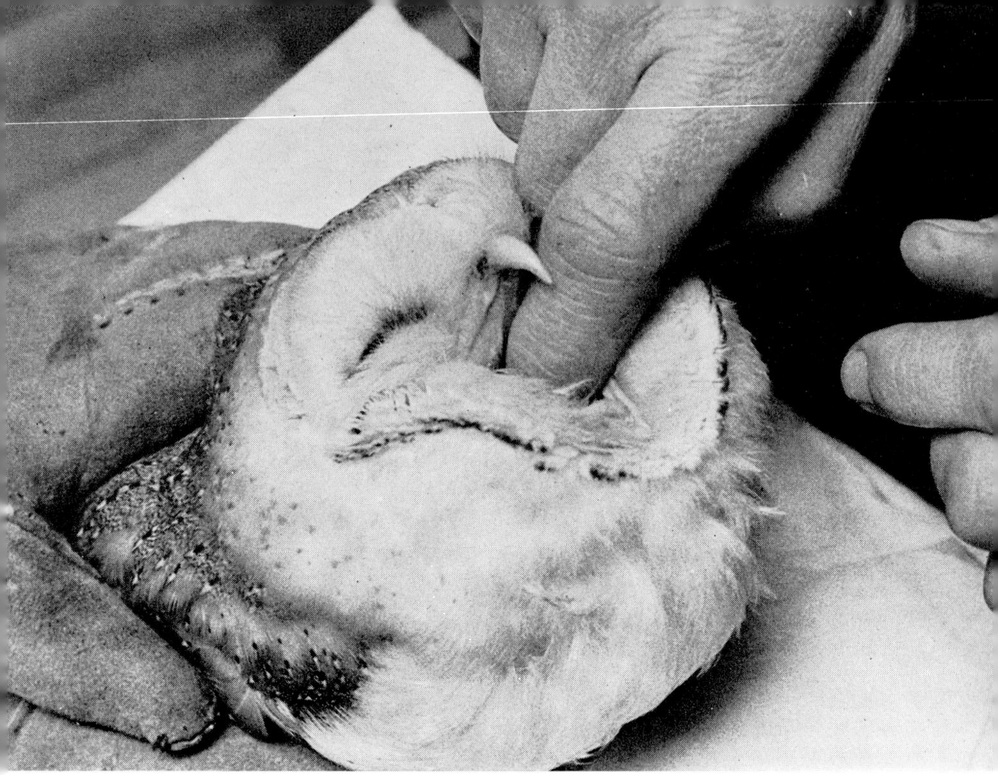

To keep him alive, the little barn owl is forced-fed until he will feed himself

Barney spread his wings and made hostile noises when confronted with a camera

hazards, and we could only hope that he had learned his lesson the hard way.

I stopped the car in a little lane close to the spot where he had been found, and in the faint light I could just see across the wide sweep of a nearby airfield which has been used continually since the war for paratroop training. I guessed that he would know this area well, being an ideal place for a barn owl to hunt, and when I lifted him from his box in the car I pointed him in this direction. Whether or not he immediately recognized where we were I did not know, but he opened his wings and suddenly the weight was gone from my hands. For a second I thought he was going to crash into the hedge which separated the adjoining field from the lane, but in the same way that I had witnessed before in the lounge, he hesitated, on moth-like wings, lifted easily up over the hedge and then swept off into the night. We stood staring for some minutes into the dim light which had engulfed him, but he was gone. He was equipped for this environment and we were not; the darkness and evening chill closed around us; we were as vulnerable as the prey he would be feeding on that night. He was the master, and with these thoughts we returned to the car and the journey home.

It had been a brief encounter, compared with many of the birds we had kept but he was a very memorable bird and one which will stand out in my mind long after others have been forgotten.

11

Late arrivals

Misty and Blackie were only two of many arrivals that year, as more and more people became aware of our activities. Friends arriving at the house would never attempt to go from one room to another without first enquiring if they would be disturbing any new occupant – even the bathroom had to be used in emergencies. One of my friends, Trevor, was always prepared to give up his garage, specializing mainly in tawny owls. But my first collared dove never really stayed with us; he came in for a thorough check after being hit by a car and then enjoyed the next fortnight with Trevor, eventually setting up territory in his back garden and taking food placed on the garage roof in preference to finding his own. A large proportion of the birds, however, are short-stay visitors and somehow we manage to fit them all in.

Some are naturally more demanding than others, and the birds which interfere with my timetable most, with the exception of the very tiny birds, are the thrushes, for I have to go out late each evening, armed with torch and dish, to catch worms on the lawn after they have emerged for the night. This generally necessitates waiting until about eleven-thirty pm in the summer, which makes bed-time rather late. Not showing any concern for my welfare, the birds are demanding attention again at about six am or earlier, and therefore my sleeping hours are, to say the least, severely restricted. Just to ensure that the few hours spent in bed are not entirely uninterrupted, Olly II returns at first light to the accompaniment of a cacophony from the blackbirds in the garden, as he invariably makes his arrival at the bedroom window, which he enters if it is sufficiently open. Then he comes on to the pillow to pull gently at my hair as if asking me to get up and let him go downstairs to the living-room where he will spend the rest of the day. I have often tried to dissuade him from this practice, leaving the bathroom window wide open and closing the bedroom window in the hope that he might wait in the bathroom until I get up to let him into the living-room, but all attempts have failed and now I automatically wake up at first light even if he has decided to spend the night in, which he occasionally does if the weather is inclement.

Very early in July, following an unusually long dry spell when catching worms had been very difficult, we had experienced about twenty-four hours of heavy rain and therefore I had secured a good stock of worms, storing the surplus in an old zinc bath filled with soil – no more late nights for at least a week! Relishing the thought of an eight-hour sleep, we prepared for bed; feeding the dogs and birds ensures that we are not going to be ready before about eleven pm anyway, but just before the final lights out on 4 July a knock came at the door. My heart sank momentarily, the prospect of sleep fast disappearing, and when I opened the door to find a man clutching a small cardboard box I knew bed was still some way off.

He was full of apologies for the late hour, but explained that the two little house martins had been the occupants of a nest which had fallen from his neighbour's house, and his wife had been terribly worried about them but could do nothing until he had returned from night shift at one of the local factories. They were very small; five or six days old I thought, and one of them looked very dishevelled, unhappy and cold. The other looked less sorry for himself and I thought that with warmth and food he might pull through, though the weaker one would need Divine help to see the morning light again. I had prepared some· very finely-chopped liver which had been put in the refrigerator for breakfast for another little house martin which was staying with us. This was quickly brought out and warmed, whilst Joyce nestled the two little birds in her hand to raise their temperature a little. After about ten minutes we opened the beak of the stronger one and popped in a piece of liver. This is most easily achieved I find by spearing the pieces lightly on the end of a partially-sharpened matchstick. He swallowed it readily and in less than a minute he had comfortably taken half a dozen pieces. Encouraged by the immediate success we turned to the weak little fellow and, although he was prepared to co-operate, he could only manage three pieces before dropping back into my wife's hand in a deep sleep. We allowed them to rest in her hand for a further half-hour before rousing them again and, when we did, they needed only the stimulus of the sight of liver to come craning forward on wobbly necks, beaks wide open, eager to snatch off the snippets. Perhaps they would be both all right after all. They certainly did not lack the will to live and this is often ninety per cent of the problem: not that the road in front was straightforward by any means. At one o'clock, and three small feeds later, we tumbled into bed feeling exhausted and wondering what tomorrow might bring. Joyce was certainly in for a hectic spell with young thrushes, house martins and a couple of owls to contend with, but if I found myself waiting for a meal occasionally I knew that they would not, and we had learned to accept that sort of thing as normal.

I did not bother to change the alarm clock, knowing that I would check them when Olly II came back at about four-fifteen am so they were placed in a tiny camera box, well padded with tissues and with a couple of tissues over them for a bedspread, and put in the warm kitchen until morning. Olly's timing was true to the minute, but it was not until he had pulled heartily at my hair that I emerged from a deep sleep and with weariness in all of my bones, I crawled rather reluctantly from bed. I think part of my reluctance stemmed from the subconscious fear that I was going to enter the kitchen to find one of the house martins dead. There was little else I could have done, but I still feel deeply guilty if we register a loss under these sort of circumstances. Nothing stirred when I switched on the light and my heart sank – surely not both of them. I lifted the tissue, which still remained just as it had been placed earlier, and four little black eyes blinked in unison, then, as one, two heads popped up with beaks held wide open, ready for the party to begin. Party – I had not even baked a cake or, for that matter, given much thought for morning at all.

A fly buzzed by, and on closer inspection I could see three more on the wall above the boiler – they would help. Fly-swatting at such an unearthly hour is very much a hit or miss affair, and I soon decided that a few small mealworms would do just as well and they could be secured with far less effort. They had not eaten all of the liver either, and I thought a *pâté* of crushed mealworms and liver would be adequate for an early breakfast – from the response it appeared to be generally agreed. I did not want to spend too much time with them, knowing that the alarm clock was set for six-thirty am to give me time to prepare worms for the thrushes, breakfast for the house martins and still have time to wash and shave before leaving for work. They were very co-operative though, and ate greedily before each in turn swivelled round, shuffled to the edge of the 'nest' and excreted over the side; all very sanitary. The droppings were contained in a thick white sac, which could easily be picked up without breaking, and they appeared very normal, which again gave me great encouragement. Having fed and emptied their bowels, they tucked into the back of the box and settled to sleep.

When I returned to bed I felt much happier about their future and before dropping off to sleep again I planned how to improve their 'nest' which they had accepted so well; they obviously needed the packing material higher on the front lip to enable them to excrete without standing on their heads (a position gained with some difficulty with the present set-up), and by angling the box, the back end could be given depth for them to nestle in for sleep. A piece of tissue to catch the droppings would complete a very convenient home for them (see sketch). For how long this arrangement would be adequate we could only speculate but there was little value in looking too far into the future and, although I felt extremely tired, I was anxious to get up again to make the necessary modifications to see how well it would work out. I hoped it would prove to be a convenient arrangement and, with some food in a saucer beside them, they could have a small feed whenever they demanded. In the event they demanded almost constantly and Joyce found herself flitting from one group of hungry birds to the next and then back again without let-up. This meant that everything else had to be marked down a few places on the list of priorities, in the faint hope that one day we could catch up on the non-essentials like mowing the lawn, or cleaning the windows, or the host of other jobs which my wife insists must be done but which I try to ignore at times like this.

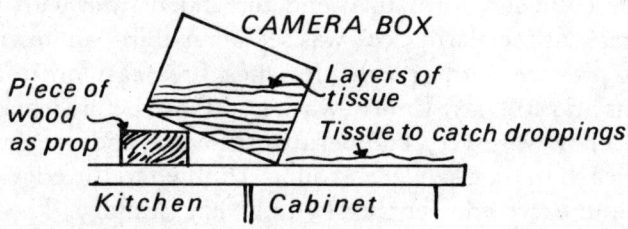

The system worked like a charm; the nest was not fouled, which meant that the birds remained scrupulously clean; they could be fed easily and efficiently; and even the temperature could be controlled by opening or closing the kitchen window which was nearby. Many of the fears which had haunted me earlier had already vanished and, with the previous experience we had gained by feeding swifts, swallows and other house martins, we felt fairly confident of success. Through the day Joyce maintained a constant supply of liver, adding a few houseflies and mealworms as the time allowed; by night both birds were looking much stronger and had settled down extremely well, accepting their new surroundings as if they had hatched in the box; brooded of course by my wife.

When I arrived in the kitchen at about four-fifteen am the next morning I lifted the tissue with far less apprehension and was greeted by two hungry mouths and a great deal of excited chatter. My first concern, after the initial worries, came when they both turned about to complete their toiletries and I noticed that their droppings were a bit loose. They were still contained in the white envelope, but I suspected that the diet which had sustained several older birds for quite long periods was not entirely suited to this tiny pair and therefore, after consultation with Joyce, we decided to switch from liver to lean beef, and add more flies and mealworms to the menu. The change of diet soon rectified the problem but, with a short holiday approaching, I felt that an effort should be made to secure a more natural diet, at least for a few days, to ensure sound progress through this very critical period.

Quite how I was to acquire a natural diet and in sufficient quantity I did not know, because in the past I had always considered this to be totally impracticable and therefore had never tried. I was not even sure what a truly natural diet would be, but from careful observations of the birds flying over my garden, they appeared to catch flying insects in a purely random manner, taking anything which came into close contact. Occasionally they would correct suddenly in flight to take an insect large enough to see through my binoculars and therefore I assumed that, with the exception of large bees and butterflies, anything else would be acceptable. The only problem which remained was how to catch them.

My young son, Alan, had recently purchased a small plastic net with which he intended to catch minnows, and the garden seemed to house a great variety of winged insects so, confident that I could hunt down the prey with the equipment at hand, I ventured out to begin my fly-catching holiday. To say that my early attempts were not very encouraging would certainly not overstate the case. I could get the odd fly in, but its reactions were quicker than mine and escape became almost inevitable. In utter disgust, after about an hour's unsuccessful thrashing around with the net, I plonked the net firmly over a fly which was sunning itself on the garden seat and it immediately flew up into the top of the net, buzzing around in confusion but not attempting to fly back down on to the seat. Intrigued by this I lifted the net up, still holding it in the inverted position and still the fly remained in the net. Eureka!

Soon I was deftly dropping the net over small clusters of flies, which could be transported back to a newspaper placed on the lawn, where I could kill the flies between thumb and finger whilst still in the net and drop the remains on to the paper. I found the newspaper to be a necessary part of the equipment as any flies falling on the lawn were lost for ever. As I gained in proficiency I found that I could sit comfortably on the seat and catch almost anything which settled within a radius of about six feet. My holiday suddenly took on a much more relaxed air, and I had a ready excuse that more flies were needed whenever I felt like sitting in the sun. Even so I found it extremely difficult to keep pace with them and, although a hundred good-sized flies would be sufficient to change the high-pitched hunger cries to a more subdued level, and they would even sleep for a few minutes after such a feed, I had only to pick up the matchbox for them to be craning forward, calling expectantly for the next batch. During my first day of fly-catching they consumed a hundred and seventy-five various winged insects, from large blue-bottles to very small flies, and this had to be supplemented with finely chopped beef (two pieces about the size of a walnut through the day). If this, then, was their rate of consumption at a relatively early age, what would they build up to?

I was anxious at first as to what effect this diet would have upon them, because there was no way in which I could be certain that I was catching the right types of insect. Everything appeared to be satisfactory but, as a further cautionary measure, my wife and I visited the local woods where many hirundines can be found feeding over the lake which is situated among the trees, and we thought we would be able to gain a fairly accurate idea of the flies being taken. Armed with the net we ventured out on to a fallen tree, amid the clouds of insects swarming over the water, and watched the martins make their assault flights among them. This time we felt certain that it was a question of mouth-open and hope for the best, because the flight was direct and lacked the erratic jinking which we had noted whilst watching them over the garden. All we had to do was to wield our giant-sized martin-mouth and we would have a truly representative sample of food. This, in fact, proved to be less positive than we had hoped, because many of the really small insects were either not caught at all or escaped before we could secure them, but at least we had a partial answer, and although the fly species were generally smaller than I had been feeding them, I could see nothing wrong with the insects I had been catching in the garden and I felt happy about continuing.

When we arrived back from the lake, albeit we had only been gone about an hour, the little martins were clamouring for food and I decided to give them a hearty feed of beef to keep them going whilst I went out, yet again, in quest of insects. Whether they had become too hungry, or whether I had stuffed them too full of beef too quickly, I shall never know but I was horrified when the stronger one began to gape in a most distressing manner and saliva bubbled from his mouth, filling his nostrils and soon covering his whole face. I quickly swabbed away the fluid with a tissue, and even soaked up some of the excess in his throat in the same way, but I felt deeply guilty about leaving them for so long and almost prayed that I had not done irreparable damage. The other had not reacted in this way and therefore I felt that he would probably recover, but it clearly illustrated how easily things can go wrong and, as I have said before, only attention to detail can ever breed success. I am sure I had allowed complacency to creep in, thinking that they would cope with a short period of starvation and the subsequent heavy meal without problems.

I brooded over the matter whilst catching flies in the garden, and determined there and then that they would not be kept for long periods without food and, as far as possible, that that food would be flies. Fortunately the young one had recovered completely when I returned with the catch, and fought alongside the other for his share of the quarry. Probably my damaged conscience had sharpened my reflexes because by nightfall they had eaten 300 flies between them, representing, I estimated, the equivalent of no less than 1500 to 1800 of the type flying over the lake, which meant that an average brood of four would be demanding that their parents catch them well over 3,000 insects a day – and that before considering their own requirements. When one considers, even in these rough terms, the insects collected by a colony of house martins, not to mention the other insect-eaters, it is easy to see the tremendous impact this must have on the insect populations and, indeed, on our own lives.

Having taken a good feed they would preen themselves and scratch out some of the downy fluff which still protruded in little tufts, before settling down for a short nap. At the first sign of movement, however, they were up on their toes again and, if food was not forthcoming, it was not long before they were fighting. At first we thought that this was merely good-humoured play, but when the smaller one actually pulled a few feathers from the crown of the other it became clear that the play was not entirely harmless. He became so persistent in his attacks that we nicknamed him Scrapper – he typified the back-street hooligan in every way, his eyes gleaming, two tufts of feathers sticking up, one on either side of his head, like the devil himself; the recipient of these attacks, because of his constant squeaks, we called Squeaker. The fights often looked worse than they really were, and generally there had been no harm done when eventually they tired and settled down to sleep again. As soon as their eyes were shut they took on a positively angelic look and even Scrapper appeared incapable of mischief of any kind.

By now at my estimation they were about eleven to twelve days old, and I was extremely pleased with their progress. I was surprised, however, by the marked difference in plumage colouration. When they had first arrived, Scrapper had appeared dirty and generally dishevelled and therefore I did not think that there was any other significance in the fact that they were not identical in appearance. But, as the days went by and new feathers grew, it was obvious that Scrapper was growing grey feathers where Squeaker, and any other house martins I had ever seen, had white. The fluffy, powder-puff feathers which froth out along the base of the closed wing in the young birds were as white as drifted snow on Squeaker, whereas with Scrapper they were the most lovely smoke-grey. Similarly his throat and upper breast feathers were also grey and even his underparts were not the pure white one would expect. When the sun shone on their backs the highlights of green and purple could be seen on both birds, but Scrapper's head was much duller, with the black merging delicately into grey behind the eyes and eventually fusing into the smoke-grey chin. As far as I was concerned he was unique – charming, demanding, even aggressive, he had the qualities which immediately command respect and affection.

Unfortunately his aggressive nature developed at the expense of Squeker and it soon became apparent that, although we could ensure that they both had their fair share of food, Squeaker was withdrawing into himself and becoming a nervous introvert. I was reluctant to separate them, but there was little alternative if Squeaker was to survive, and therefore we made use of a large cardboard box which was divided into halves by a partition, and in each we made a 'nest', leaving an area for them to come out into to feed. To this we added a perch which was, in fact, a piece of stout electric cable stretched taut about two inches off the bottom of the box. Because we had only one camera box and nothing else of similar size, we used soup dishes for the nests and these, in fact, proved ideal. I think it is true to say that they missed each other's company at first, but they settled down well and we felt much happier about their welfare.

We had had them now for ten days, their progress had been excellent, and we were naturally reluctant to change any part of the successful routine. Fly-catching on days when the weather was cool and windy was becoming a chore, and I had to employ the children who were, at the time, on summer holidays from school. At ten pence per 500 flies, their pocket money could be valuably increased and the house martins were assured of a steady supply. I continued to take my turn and had often netted the first hundred before anyone else had emerged from bed – in fact, I found that the first rays of sun which lit the dew on the leaves of the alders at the bottom of my garden attracted a number of insects, including many large blow-flies, which were always taken readily and were encouraging to catch as they quickly filled the matchbox.

After a couple of days of 'solitary confinement' the martins began to flutter up on top of the dividing partition and they would chatter and look inquisitively at one another, but in no time at all they were back together again, often sharing each other's accommodation and I was greatly intrigued by their change of attitude. It would be untrue to state that there were no further skirmishes, but they never displayed any real aggression after their parting and, as Squeker had apparently recovered his confidence, we decided to give them a much larger box to share and subsequently they could be found either sitting close beside each other on the perch or nestled happily in one of the soup dishes. After the last feed in the evening, however, each always returned to his own nest and would resist any attempt by the other to occupy it. I had ample opportunity to verify this behaviour, and they returned to the same dish throughout their stay with as much certainty as if they had their own front door keys. I began to worry slightly about this particular evening ritual because, if house martins return to their nests at night to roost, often cramming it to overflowing as subsequent broods are produced but resisting occupation by others, where would Scrapper and Squeaker roost after release? I try not to worry too much about problems before they actually occur, but in this case I could see no ready solution despite pondering the problem most evenings at bed-time. In the event, we made the best compromise without success, but that is leaping ahead too far for the moment.

As soon as they realized the world was larger than a cardboard box, the martins were anxious to explore it, and a kitchen, so warm and comforting for those which are securely tucked down in a 'nest', is fraught with hazards for venturesome young birds. By necessity the cooker has to be too hot for little feet, washing-up bowls are no place to bathe in, and hot irons are hardly satisfactory mirrors in which to pander to one's vanity, no matter how well preened and pleased with the day's turn-out. To give them freedom in safety we agreed that they must be moved to another room, but first we decided to limit their activities during danger periods when cooking and washing-up were in progress by covering the top of the box with polythene and then liberating them for a fly round when they could be watched, mainly in the evening. For two or three days this worked extremely well and they very soon became proficient in flight, finding all the best resting-places, and they became capable of quite complicated manoeuvres to avoid any obstacles. They did not appear to object to comparative confinement during the day, and it was very amusing to watch them dispatch the flies which were placed in the box because by now, although we still hand-fed the beef, we tipped a matchbox full of flies on to the bottom of their box and they hopped down from the perch and shuffled around on little feathery legs, pecking up the flies in a manner reminiscent of chickens pecking up grain. The big problem was still catching enough flies to satisfy their needs but we persisted and only had to resort to beef two or three times a day.

Although the kitchen arrangement had proved to be highly successful to bring them to the stage where they could fly, we did not feel happy that they could be turned out into the world with so little experience in sustained flight and so we decided to transport their box into the lounge each morning, having left them for the night secure in their polythene-covered box in the warm kitchen. The lounge presented none of the hazards which would undoubtedly have led to disaster in the kitchen and it was much larger, giving them real space to test their wings. Because they had become used to perching on the heavy electric cable, which we had used throughout, I stretched a similar length across the lounge, only this time about five feet from the ground, from which they could launch themselves and then return to rest and preen. They were naturally a bit suspicious of their new surroundings at first, but it was not long before they were flying around with gay abandon, obviously enjoying their new-found talents, and we felt strongly that we should plan immediately for their release.

One thing we had decided to do was to place rings on their legs (not my normal practice) so that there would be a possibility, albeit very remote, that we might subsequently learn of their success, or failure, in the world outside. Trevor, the spare-garage owner and very good friend of mine, gave Scrapper the unique distinction of wearing ring number JK 24829 and on Squeaker he bestowed ring number JK 24828. The ceremony was completed on 23 July, 1974, and within minutes of being ringed they were happily flying around the lounge to their, and everyone else's, delight.

It had been a testing time for all concerned for their welfare over the past nineteen days, but it was generally agreed that they were ready for the off. Several points of concern had been resolved as well as could be expected. Flies dangled on the end of a length of cotton were readily snapped up when swung in pendulum fashion past their noses as they sat on the wire. Even free-flying flies which ventured in were closely followed by four bright eyes, but they needed more space and fewer obstacles to fly them down as prey and we were happy that, given their true environment, they would accomplish that with a little practice. They were also beginning to show distinct interest in the world beyond the window and could often be found sitting on the window-sill, gazing into the sky where swallows and other house martins were wheeling in their constant search for food. True, we had not resolved the problem of where they were going to roost after they had left home, but we could think of nothing better than fixing their roosting box against the wall beside the kitchen window, to which they could return in comparative safety if they so chose. We knew all too well that the eventual release would be accompanied by all the agonies experienced so often before, but there was no legitimate reason for delay and therefore the prospect had to be faced as unemotionally as possible. That evening we discussed the timing of the release and, having decided that they should go some time during the next day, we thought that we should feed them up to capacity during the morning and then launch them on their way about lunch-time.

The next morning dawned grey and overcast and, when I ventured out at six o'clock to collect the first batch of flies, a fine drizzle enveloped me. The first rays of sun were certainly not going to light the dew on the alders this side of lunch-time; in fact, the stiff, cool breeze which was beating the fine rain against my face was going to ensure that most insects would stay in hiding until the weather improved. After an hour spent vainly looking for flies, the bottom of the matchbox contained only half a dozen soggy offerings. So much for feeding them up prior to release! We could easily substitute beef of course, but conditions were hardly ideal for their first sally into the world beyond, and by lunch-time both Joyce and I had independently arrived at the same conclusion. Scrapper and Squeaker remained aloof from all the tension and spent a busy and contented day in the lounge and, with the promise of better weather the next day, a short delay appeared incidental. When we went to bed at night we speculated about where they might have been, had not the weather intervened in our plans, and we eventually convinced ourselves that everything had turned out for the best because we would have felt sick with worry if they had been forced to face adverse conditions immediately after release. Therefore the sleep which effectively terminated our speculations after a short while was both deep and contented. As is so often the case with our English weather, the sun shone the next morning in brilliant contrast to the day before and before my head lifted from the pillow I could hear the lively calls

143

of swallows and martins quartering their aerial territories, obviously as pleased with the change as I was.

Throughout the period the house martins had been with us we had also been coping with three very young song thrushes whose parents had been killed by a cat, and it would be wrong to pretend that there was not some measure of relief at the thought of the house martins flying away to find their own food on this bright, sunny day. As I entered the living-room I received a soft hoot as a greeting from Olly II and popped my head into the bathroom to be heralded by a full chorus from the thrushes which were, by now, almost ready for the off themselves. Feeling positively elated, I entered the kitchen where I knew the friendly chirping of the house martins would accompany my first job of the day: preparing coffee for Joyce and myself, which I usually sipped in comfort whilst smoking a pipe of tobacco after having washed and shaved. As soon as my hand fell on the door knob I knew something was wrong. An empty silence filled the room. I rushed to the box and peered in and was totally unable to believe what I saw. Squeker and Scrapper were lying on the bottom of the box quite motionless. I picked them up and they were unable to lift their heads off the palm of my hand. They were alive – just, but they felt cold and I was sure, very near to death. My immediate thoughts lacked coherence but I closed my hands around them hoping that the warmth would revive them a little and called Joyce to the scene. I had not been out to catch any flies, so after a while we attempted to give them a few tiny snippets of beef but even when it was placed right down their throats they were unable to swallow it and I felt utterly useless. In the faint hope that flies would be more acceptable I left Joyce in charge whilst I went into the garden with the net. Never have I felt such abject misery, and I was so absolutely deflated by the situation that I experienced difficulty in catching flies – it all seemed so pointless anyway. I returned quickly with the first few I had caught, anxious to test their reaction, and although they could only accept one at a time at least they managed to get something

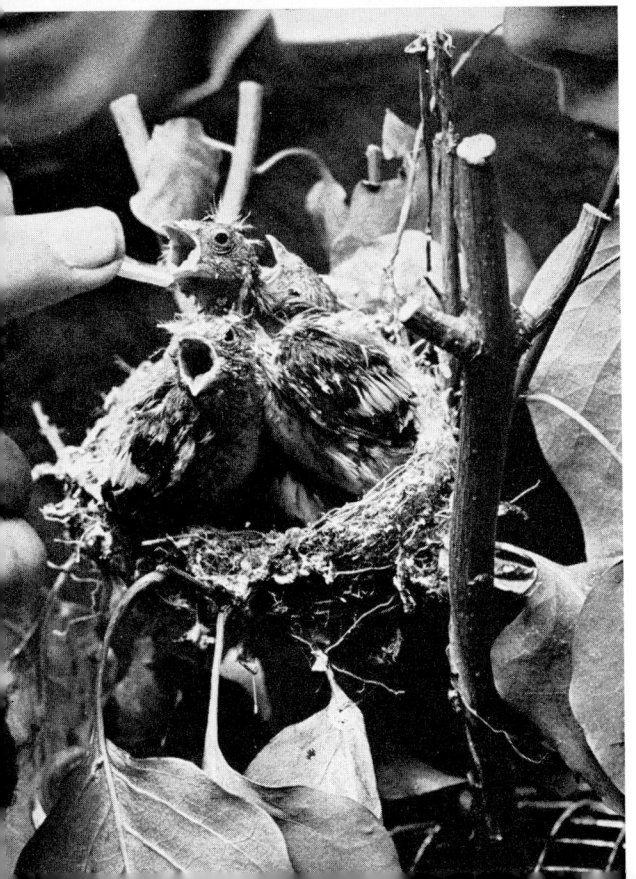

Unlike an owl, a kestrel removes fur or feathers before tearing at the meat

Baby goldfinches are fed a mixture of breakfast cereal, glucose, vitamins and water from a matchstick

Katie the kestrel: hit by a car, she recovered health
and confidence in her temporary foster-home

inside them. It was whilst we were giving them flies we noticed that the inside of their mouths and their tongues were thickly coated white, almost like a fungal growth, so different from the night before when the electric light had shone clearly through the membrane behind the lower mandible, and little pink tongues had flicked anxiously as they anticipated the next piece of meat.

Calamities are unfortunately all too commonplace at home, but this was so sudden and so dramatic that I felt nothing but utter despondency. What were the possible explanations? The meat, which we bought in small amounts from the butcher each day to ensure a fresh supply, had been fed to them throughout and therefore there could be no connection there. Flies were certainly a much more questionable ingredient of the diet because of their habit of feeding and laying eggs on possibly contaminated carrion, or coming into contact with dangerous and sometimes lethal sprays. The only other alternative that I could think of was the possibility that they might have contracted some viral disease. Whatever the cause, however, we had to take positive action, and although they were looking a little brighter they were certainly not going to recover by eating the odd fly every half an hour or so. It was crystal clear that we would have to switch, at least temporarily, to a liquid diet to get their strength back and also, if they had picked up a virus, perhaps a course of antibiotics would be the answer. I mixed 1 ml of Epivax with 20 mls water, and to this I added a spot of Abidec multi-vitamin drops and 2 mls glucose. To each in turn we gave a few drops from the end of a matchstick, and then we wrapped them up warm beside the boiler. After a few minutes we gave them another few drops apiece, and they appeared relieved when the liquid ran down their throats, swallowing readily. I had to leave Joyce to cope whilst I went off to work and I knew she felt the burden of responsibility very heavy upon her.

The morning dragged on like eternity, not knowing what was happening at home, but when lunch-time arrived I was pleased to find them looking much brighter. They were sitting together in one of the soup dish nests looking rather fluffed out and dejected, but at least they were on their feet, and as well as eagerly taking fluid (which I had mixed earlier) all morning, they were able to cope with the odd fly which the children had caught. There was still no way of telling whether the treatment would be successful or not, but at least we had arrested the condition and for that we felt extremely relieved. Lunch was a more than usual scratch meal, Joyce having done nothing but tend to the house martins' needs all morning, but when I returned to work I was much more optimistic again. As I came home in the evening I hardly dared think of their fate, but steady progress had been maintained throughout the day and they were even keeping pace with the supply of flies which the children were working hard to maintain. To give my wife a break I took over the feeding duties, and was happy in the fact that it was difficult to find sufficient flies to contain their hunger. At about eleven pm they settled for sleep and, although I intended to check them regularly through the night, I thought it better that they should be allowed to rest quietly if they wished.

The day had been a living nightmare, impossible to describe. Exaggerated as it may seem in retrospect, if one of the children had been taken seriously ill I do not think that at the time we could have felt more concerned, because although I have always tried to remain unemotional about the birds we care for, these were as close to us as our own kind. From their initial emergence from the eggs to their arrival at our home, had only been a few hours, and we had watched their development proudly, feeling the elation that they must surely have felt when their wings spread in earnest for the first time and took them into the element that was to be their future home. We had thought about the terrifying journey south that they would have to undertake in the autumn, and had speculated about the birds, other animals and people that they would see in Africa before, hopefully, they would seek this tiny part of England again next spring to return to and breed.

After the initial worries about their condition, we had never looked upon losing them as a possibility, and we went to bed that night, quite stunned by the disastrous events of the day. Unlike me, they slept through the night, and although they had lost a little ground by morning, they were able to feed on flies and little snippets of meat which were first dipped in Epivax solution. During the day a friend brought in a rabbit which had been killed on the road and asked if the meat would be useful for one of the three owls which we had at the time. We were always extremely grateful for such offerings because, apart from the colossal butcher's bill which we inevitably had to meet (despite his generosity) they afforded more natural diet with a ready supply of roughage. I had always given this type of food to the larger birds of prey or carrion eaters, but it struck me that rabbit meat might be more readily digestible than beef and therefore we decided to try the house martins with a few finely-chopped pieces. To enable them to swallow the meat more easily, we dipped each piece into Epivax solution, thus ensuring that they had their quota of antibiotics, and did not over-exert themselves whilst feeding. The immediate response was very encouraging, more so when I later examined the droppings and found them to be looser, with fully digested waste being passed, which compared favourably with the rather dry droppings they had excreted since their illness and which had contained undigested particles of flies and meat. All the indications were that they were extracting the goodness from the food, and with antibiotics and vitamins added I could see no reason why their progress should not be maintained or even improved. This, happily, proved to be the case.

It was four days before they took to the wing again. They were both sitting on Joyce's lap after a feed when Squeaker, having preened, flapped wildly and then flew confidently across to the settee. It was a flight of only about four feet, but he had felt sufficiently well to attempt to fly and we rated this as a big step forward. Scrapper had also become very excited by all the sudden activity, but on reflection he decided to perform a few taxi-ing manoeuvres to ensure everything was in good order before the actual flight and, after running up his engines several times, he was too exhausted to get airborne and settled, instead, for a short nap on his foster-mother's knee.

For the first time in several days I was greeted the next morning by excited chatter from within their box, and during the day they both flew several sorties around the kitchen. We prayed that nothing would go wrong this time but we had to give them a few more days in the lounge to ensure that they had the stamina to maintain a fully active day. One can feel quite fit when resting in bed following a bout of 'flu, but the feeling changes dramatically when one gets up and attempts a normal day, and, although I was anxious that they should be allowed to take up their place in the wild as soon as possible, I did not want to jeopardize their chances by releasing them too soon.

As the days passed and their strength increased, we judged that we could probably release them on Tuesday, 6 August. I was keen on this idea because I finished work at midday, Tuesday being the early closing day for our shops, and therefore I would have the opportunity of observing their reaction in the wild, always assuming, of course, that they would join the other house martins which were feeding close to home.

When the day dawned I felt sure that we had chosen well, and when I went into the garden, birds and insects were all busily engaged in securing food. This time the martins were clamouring for food on my return and had eaten the first hundred flies before Joyce appeared in the kitchen for her coffee. We were tempted to liberate them right away, but after a short discussion we decided to adhere to the original plan, with Joyce feeding them as much as they could consume during the morning. I found her still busily engaged on this when I returned home at lunch-time. They were sitting on the towel rack in the kitchen eagerly taking pieces of rabbit which she was administering on the end of a matchstick. My wife said that they had spent a good deal of the morning gazing out of the window, fluttering their wings as if excited at the prospect of putting them to real purpose outside with the others of their

kind, and so, without delay, I set about moving their box outside the window whilst Joyce finished feeding them.

I opened the window in preparation, and with hardly a
moment's hesitation Scrapper was out – low across the lawn,
then buoyantly over the little wall which parts the garden from
the field below, and then in a tremendous sweep skyward to join
the others. I rushed out with my binoculars and was just in time
to see Squeaker hurtle through the window, feel the wind in his
wings and then rise almost vertically to about a hundred feet.
He flew straight to one of the many adults and they fluttered
momentarily face to face before falling away and then wheeling
back into the milling crowd. I watched Squeaker for some minutes before I lost him in the general commotion, and then
shouted excitedly as I picked up Scrapper. His tail had formed
irregularly, one side growing better than the other and his silhouette against the deep blue sky was unmistakable. I followed
him as he swept in a wide circle over the field, and although I
could not see him catch anything, from his erratic jinking I was
certain that he was at least trying to catch insects. The next half
an hour or so that we spent lying on the lawn in the sun, gazing
skyward, must certainly rate as one of the happiest experiences
of my life. They were in a different world to us now, we could
not hope to follow them, nor had we any further part in their
lives. They could not plan, or predict, they must follow their instincts wherever they took them; over lands and oceans which
we could never hope to see. We could only watch happily as
they wheeled in bliss above us.

To conclude the practical details, we erected their box
securely against the wall by the kitchen window but as darkness
fell it became apparent that we had seen the last of our little
friends, and with cautious optimism we trudged wearily up to
bed.

12

Some useful observations

Our first introduction into the care of sick, injured or orphaned birds had stemmed from a previous interest in them and people's blind faith that we could cope with bird problems beyond normal abilities. Over the years, two main factors have come to light: that initially we had little *real* knowledge of birds and that a deeper look into their behaviour, character and general qualities presents a fascinating study. Through the earlier pages of this book I have dealt with a few experiences we have shared with birds which have been our companions for several weeks or months, and have only mentioned in passing the 'short-stay' visitors, mainly because many of the things we have learned from them could be included within the context of the stories already set down.

The time spent with the birds at home, the actual physical time spent in feeding, nursing, preparing food, cleaning and making adequate accommodation for them, is only a small portion of the time involved in getting to know the birds better in the hope of improving our methods of care. A great deal of time has to be spent, necessarily I consider, in watching carefully everything they do so that we can get at least a hint of their individual reaction to the treatment they are being subjected to, in an attempt to establish what can only be termed a 'standard behaviour' against which to judge other individuals. This will tell me roughly what to expect in captivity, but 'my' birds are destined for the wild and must learn many things if they are to survive. Close observation of adult birds can give a very good indication of what particular species are capable of and therefore we have to ensure, as far as possible, that the young ones which are raised by us have these same capabilities before they are turned out to fend for themselves.

This, then, is one small avenue to explore in order to obtain a better understanding, but observations must take place beyond the confines of one's home if a complete picture is to be established. The complete picture eludes the most dedicated student of course and I often see the problem as one enormous jigsaw puzzle: first spread at random on the table, resembling nothing but a jumble of pieces of cardboard. Gradually a few pieces are fitted into the giant mosaic giving hints of the picture to come, but so often these small fragments can be most misleading, parts of the picture hanging within the general scene, and serious modifications to earlier theories must often be made as the true picture emerges. At first there is little of interest, one can read on the packet what the contents are (much as we could readily identify the local birds we saw around home) but the excitement stems from unravelling the puzzle oneself and working towards the ultimate thrill of seeing the final creation in all its glory. I have never witnessed the final creation but occasionally I have completed sufficient of the mosaic to know that the small portion I am looking at is as the creator intended me to see it, and then I can start to feel the thrill of accomplishment.

Sometimes chance observations can be more instructive than those carefully sought, as when I watched a family of song thrushes on my garden path whilst helping Joyce with the washing up. It was a particularly dry summer and I had watered the lawn generously in order to catch worms more easily in the evening and this, in turn, had helped out the local blackbirds and thrushes, which were having a hard time finding sufficient food for the young. I had not realized, but the previous evening the sprinkler had moistened the border beside the lawn which housed a little patch of irises and this was where a large number of snails had congregated. Having three young to contend with and finding a ready supply of snails recently activated among the irises, the adult thrush decided to instruct her young in the art of snail smashing.

The youngsters peered inquisitively as their mother (or father) scratched among the tangled roots and their looks were of sheer disbelief when she emerged with a large garden snail and proceeded to whack it heartily on one of the paving stones. Having extracted the juicy interior in a very professional manner, she went up to one of the enquiring young and thrust it into his beak. His reaction was immediate: with a deft flick of his head he had thrown the snail some two feet away. Undaunted she hopped across and picked it up, first wiping it in the soil to remove the slime which the snail was emitting in defence, and repeated the process. This time the youngster managed to throw it even further away. It was more like someone putting the shot than learning to eat a snail. She picked it up without any sign of annoyance and went straight to the youngster but this time she pushed it much further down his throat. This seemed to increase his ability to throw it even further – as a shot putter he was definitely improving! The whole process was repeated fifteen times before the youngster actually swallowed it; I think he had tired of the ball game and could see no better way of concluding it than to swallow the ball.

Throughout the whole episode the other two youngsters had watched wide-eyed, probably fearing that their turn would be next. Whatever the youngsters' reaction, however, the adult intended to persist and went straight back to the iris patch to seek out another snail. Three heads craned forward to watch this extraordinary behaviour – I wondered if they were trying to determine which of them would be the recipient next time. As soon as the snail was finally beaten from its shell, it was taken to be cleaned in the soil and by now both Joyce and I were eager to see whether she would continue the lesson with the first youngster or start from scratch with another. In the event she went straight back to the first young one and rammed the snail firmly down his throat. It was an acquired taste obviously, but equally obvious was the fact that it did not take long to acquire it because he immediately threw back his head and swallowed it readily. She was infected with success and rushed back to find another snail, though this time she only partially removed the shell and stood back to encourage the youngster to finish the job by himself. Needless to say, with such an obstinate offspring, there was a great deal of encouragement necessary before he actually picked it up and hit it rather awkwardly and ineffectively on the stone, but persistence won through in the end and by the time the washing up was complete – several lots of hot water later – the first young was able to deal with a snail all by himself. The intriguing fact was that the parent concentrated on one youngster and we wondered whether she would have to repeat the whole process again with each one or whether they would learn by example. Like so many fascinating observations this one had an untimely conclusion, for the appearance of one of the children entering the garden from the field below sent them all scurrying away – no doubt to seek a fresh supply of snails.

I have since had the privilege of teaching several young song thrushes to deal with snails and I am not at all put off by their initial rejection. I can persist, knowing full well that I am truly emulating the techniques employed in the wild and this, of course, gives me tremendous confidence.

Similar observations can equally destroy one's confidence but the quest for information is never dull. We had housed an adult green woodpecker for a few days, brought to me only a short while after a popular feeding site had been sprayed with selective weedkiller, and I strongly suspected poisoning. She was an adorable creature, quite capable of inflicting a nasty rap on one's knuckles, but she settled very quickly in a large cardboard box into which we fitted a long, rough-barked log at an angle of forty-five degrees for her to perch on. I knew they fed on ants and their eggs, so I went straight to the local pet shop for a supply of ant eggs. They were sold in little polythene bags which were stapled to a card for display and when I enquired the price the assistant told me that they were ten pence each. I said that I had better take a pound's worth and she gave me the entire card, eyeing me suspiciously as I left the shop. I can only assume that the woodpecker had never seen ant eggs in a little dish before, but she immediately recognized them as food and took them readily. A few days later my wife and I took an evening stroll to an old piece of pastureland where green woodpeckers could often be found feeding, and we were overjoyed to find not one, but five; an entire family party consisting of both adults and three young. From their behaviour and appearance I judged the young to be very inexperienced, probably enjoying their first day away from the nest, and the parents were hard pressed to hold their concentration for many minutes at a time, the youngsters taking great interest in every tussock of grass instead of watching the parents digging in the ant-hills for the hidden quarry. The adult female spent several minutes hacking a hole about the size of a teacup into one of the grassy mounds and we were close enough to see through binoculars the ants moving their eggs hastily to a safer part of the nest. One had the feeling that their efforts were entirely wasted in the face of such remorseless opposition, however, and as soon as she was satisfied that sufficient had been exposed to allow the young to feed she called them over to give a first-hand demonstration of how to deal with the lively inhabitants. Unlike the little song thrushes, they immediately set about dispatching the panicking ants with deft flicks of their tongues and, in order to keep the party going, the adult hacked frantically to enlarge the hole and ensure a steady supply.

After several minutes the young decided to move on to seek out another feast, but their random pecking gave them little chance of success and they had to be called again when another ant-hill had been exposed, this time by father. How long it took before realization dawned that they must seek ants in very specific places I do not know, because despite watching them for about three-quarters of an hour they gave no hint that they had made any real progress, and we walked back pondering the possibility that some day we might have to undertake a similar job. Quite how this could be done without completely taming the birds and taking them to the real site I do not know. Fortunately, to date, I have only had to deal with adult birds, but it serves to illustrate the very real problems that must be faced if young birds are to survive after release.

It is not always young birds which present problems with feeding. Some of the adults which find their way to my house have been badly shocked or injured and are often reluctant to take food for several days; during this period it is necessary to force-feed them if they are to survive. We encountered owls before kestrels in the early days and therefore when Katie, a demure little female kestrel arrived, badly shaken by a glancing blow from a car, we felt that we could give her slightly smaller amounts of a tawny owl diet and she would be perfectly all right. Perhaps, we thought, we could err on the side of under-feeding for the first day until she settled to feed herself, but we were quite sure that she would need similar amounts of roughage to maintain a normal digestive system. However, out of caution we gave only relatively small amounts of roughage, consisting mainly of blackbird's feathers from a bird which had been killed on the road, and by doing so we unconsciously averted what could have been a serious situation. Unlike owls, kestrels and most other birds of prey have a crop, which, when the stomach is full, fills with food, thus effectively blocking the passage of a pellet and therefore it is important that they should take as little indigestible matter as possible.

As soon as Katie had recovered from the initial shock she began to feed herself, and we soon realized that her feeding habits were far removed from the owls we had watched. Our first experience of observing her coping with natural prey came when we gave her a dunnock – again a road casualty. She was a friendly little creature and in order to see clearly how she dealt with the food I gave it to her on the dining-room table: perhaps not entirely the thing to do in some households, but most things are acceptable in my house in the interests of the birds' welfare. She gripped the bird firmly with her talons and proceeded to tear out the wing and tail feathers one by one; she then removed

the majority of the feathers from the breast and back of the dunnock. By now she was standing amid a veritable mountain of
feathers, making the bird totally indistinguishable. My wife
had barely enquired, 'What will she do now?', when she stood
up on tiptoe and flapped frenziedly, scattering feathers to the
four corners of the room. She appeared completely unperturbed by the shower she had created; instead she looked
intently at the partially plucked bird. Having satisfied herself
that the meal was now ready, she tore large chunks of meat
from the breast, soon exposing the contents of the body beneath
the rib cage. It was impossible to determine exactly what she
was eating at any one time but she certainly ate the ribs along
with the meat which surrounded them. The heart, liver, some of
the gut and other choice morsels which emerged from within
were taken with obvious relish, and inside ten minutes the only
remains on the table were the two tarsi, feet and the head – later
I found that she would occasionally eat the head as well.

We were anxious, later, to see what the pellet would contain
and, to ensure that we could unravel the true picture, we gave
her only food containing no roughage until the evening when, in
fact, she duly produced a very small but interesting pellet. We
were surprised that the bones had been almost totally digested,
small parts of the upper leg remaining, and it consisted of a
compact ball of feathers surrounding the bone remains. Our
owls had always regurgitated the bones complete, quite unable
to dissolve any part of them. We had learned quite a bit about
the feeding habits by examining pellets found in the wild, but
by a complete oversight we had not been aware of this very real
difference. The moral was clear: assumption is very dangerous
and only facts should be used to determine the treatment given
to birds.

Pellets can, of course, tell a great deal about the food taken by
birds, and I was delighted to find a large hoard of carrion crow,
rook and jackdaw pellets beneath a line of fencing posts whilst
on an insect-foraging trip for the house martins. I was first
made aware of the fact that the posts were used frequently as

perches by the many white droppings deposited around the base, and it was not for some time that I realized the posts in question were used by birds which had been feeding on a nearby council refuse tip, when disturbed by the appearance of the workmen. They had used the area as a retreat and in consequence they had spent a good deal of time just sitting around waiting for the next opportunity to feed, and whilst doing so they had deposited a very fine collection of pellets.

Some of the contents were of interest but only served to demonstrate that many birds will pick up quite useless material whilst feeding: elastic bands, several pieces of aluminium foil, sweet wrappers and the like could have formed no useful part of their diet but the small stones, and even pieces of coloured glass, gave the clue to the necessity of grinding materials in the gizzard to help to break down the grass seeds which, from the large proportion of chaff present in the pellets, formed an important ingredient. Many indigestible remains of beetles were present in most of the pellets, together with a certain amount of fur, presumably from small rodents. All of the information gained only gave a very crude picture of what the birds had been feeding on because it is almost impossible to decide what proportion of easily digested material had been taken compared to the amount which had left tell-tale signs in the pellet, but at least we could compile a list of acceptable foods, and if these were given in reasonable quantities the birds could use their own discretion. Having cared for several members of the crow family, I can only conclude that the list compiled in this way falls short of the general requirements and one must add such items as earthworms, leatherjackets, lean meat, crushed cereals and, of course, fresh water. But it forms a very useful guide and at least indicated the one essential ingredient which would be most easily overlooked: namely the small stones for grinding.

Having cared for many tawny owls, we were keen to see at first hand what food they fed to their young and just how they prepared the food in the early stages. Short of putting a hide up to a nest and watching continually, always assuming that a sufficiently exposed nest could be found to allow this, there was no ready answer, but several clues were revealed when, fairly recently, we visited a nest site which contained one egg showing signs of hatching, alongside a very newly hatched young. We were naturally anxious to leave the site quickly so that the parents could return and supervise the family at such a critical stage of development, but a couple of days later we went back to find how things were progressing. The two young were sitting in the gloom of the nest, which was tucked away in a large cavity of an old chestnut tree, peering suspiciously at the entrance hole and they immediately hissed their disapproval when they saw my head appear.

To the rear of the main nest cavity a small recess had been used as a larder and contained an adult mole, a young mole, a very small rabbit and a small shrew. None of this food had been used and obviously the parents had been able to find prey in plenty, with the young demanding very little at that stage. Several feathers were present in the nest and, together with the tarsi and feet, constituted the remains of a female chaffinch. It was obvious that the bird had been fairly thoroughly plucked and I assumed that small pieces had been torn off for the young. An equally safe assumption, I think, is that the parent had eaten the head, usually the first thing to be done after killing prey, and it may well have dealt with the larger portions containing the upper leg. There, lying in the nest, then, was sufficient to build up a very accurate picture of what prey was being taken and how it was being dealt with, but I decided to return after a few more days to try to find out how much of the rabbit had been used for food. This time an even clearer picture emerged because I found the complete skin of the rabbit, still connected to the head which had remained untouched, and also many of the larger bones. By now the young were obviously demanding more food and the nearby jackdaw colony was beginning to provide some easy prey – shown by the fact that several wing and tail feathers of recently-fledged young jackdaws were present both in the nest and scattered around the entrance.

As far as we were concerned, rabbits were probably the most easily obtained food supply but, as I have explained earlier, many of our friends bring in freshly killed birds which have been found by the roadside, and therefore from our observations we were happy in the knowledge that our owls were getting a correct diet. Experience of them in captivity has shown me that they are very fond of bathing, and I am quite sure that birds in the wild must enjoy a bath very regularly although I must confess I have yet to witness this behaviour.

During the years I have cared for birds I have grown closer and closer to an understanding of them, but the full appreciation has always sufficiently eluded me to guarantee a further lifetime of captivating study. They have given me indescribable joy, they have taught me patience and tolerance, but above all they have taught me the fascination of learning. I have felt privileged that such honest and genuine tutors have accepted me and given me a glimpse into the complex world which, fortunately, still surrounds our homes.